Speaking of Wagner:
Talking to Audiences About *The Ring of the Nibelung*

William Berger

Speaking of Wagner:
Talking to Audiences About *The Ring of the Nibelung*

William Berger

Academica Press
Washington – London

Library of Congress Cataloging-in-Publication Data
Names: Berger, William, author.
Title: Speaking of Wagner : talking to audiences about the Ring of the
Nibelung / William Berger
Description: Washington : Academica Press, 2020. | Includes index.
Identifiers: LCCN 2020934615 | ISBN 9781680530964 (hardcover) |
9781680530971 (paperback)

Contents

Acknowledgements

I am greatly indebted to many people for their time and support, and it's distressing that I can only name a few. I am especially grateful to those who continue to seek me out for engagements to speak about opera and related subjects, especially Dalia Geffen, Dr. Steven Prystowsky, Loren Toolajian, Terri Stuart, Brendan Cooke, Jeff McMillan, Dr. Benjamin Torbert, Darlene Ronald, Margarita Miranda Mitrov, and Dan Egan. All of my friends and colleagues in the New York music scene tolerate a great deal of me using them as testing grounds for ideas in addition to giving direct support to my work, but special thanks for patient, helpful, and judicious feedback go to Jason Lekberg, Sam Walters, Tom Wendol, Sandy Schuster, and Nicholas Horner. For providing places to stay and work in my travels, I'm seriously grateful to many people, especially Ramón Berger, Molly McBride, and Hubert Gonthier-Blouin (who additionally insisted we go to distant Saguenay and caused us to stumble upon an encampment where we experienced a surprise demonstration of Viking sword making, which became an essential part of this book). I wish it were possible to name all the people at the Metropolitan Opera, and especially in the media, music, and editorial departments, who are without a doubt the most excellent team of dedicated experts I've ever encountered, but for the moment I can only name Hillary Ley, Gillian Brierley, Marsha Drummond, Dr. Kamala Schelling, and Dan Marshall for their help and support with events within and beyond the Met, many of which became the basis of this book. And speaking of Vikings ... a special thanks to Paul du Quenoy for his accessibility and guidance in making this book happen. Finally, heartfelt thanks to my husband Stephen J. Miller, who not only contributed in all ways listed above, but also specifically for his intense brand of editorial assistance.

Chapter I
Talking about
Talking About *The Ring of the Nibelung*

In an act of hubris analogous to Richard Wagner's when he composed such a gigantic, megalomaniacal, unimaginably vast creation as *The Ring of the Nibelung* (the difference in scope between my folly and his being measured by the difference between his supreme and toxic genius and my small, if benign, talents), I told the management of the Metropolitan Opera that it needed someone to give talks before performances of the *Ring* in the spring of 2019 – and that I was the person to give them.

A lot was at stake, for Wagner fans and for the Met, in these performances. The work itself is a four-part "music drama." Each of its constituent parts, from the *"Vorabend"* ("preliminary evening") *Das Rheingold* to the concluding *Götterdämmerung* ("The Twilight of the Gods") is a full evening in the theater, to put it mildly. *Das Rheingold* runs about two and a half hours, depending on the conductor, with no intermission. The next parts, *Die Walküre* ("The Valkyrie") and *Siegfried,* are each about five hours with intermissions. *Götterdämmerung* pushes six hours, with its prelude and first act alone being well about two hours. It's as demanding on a company's resources and imaginations as it is on the audience's butts. Wagner dreamed of a new theater to be built according to his specifications in order to stage the first complete cycle of the work in 1876 (*Das Rheingold* and *Die Walküre* premiered separately, in 1869 and 1870, respectively), and every production of it everywhere else since then has been a major statement by that local company and even a matter of civic and national pride when accomplished well. It is simply the biggest thing in the performing arts.

The 2019 performances were the third presentation of Robert Lepage's production of the *Ring* at the Met, and the company's hope was the third time would prove the proverbial charm. The production had been introduced in installments (as is typical) from 2010 through 2012. The initial splash was not entirely successful. It was not a flop, as some insisted, but neither was it by any measure a triumph—and a production of something as expensive, cumbersome, and high-profile as the *Ring* that is not a triumph becomes something of a flop by definition. The first year left audiences simultaneously overwhelmed and underwhelmed by the central conceit: the entire work was staged on a "machine," a massive (and massively expensive) juggernaut of planks that reconfigured into various forms, sometimes quite noisily, other times not correctly, throughout the epic. Critics competed with each other for the honor of Most Venomous Denunciation of the Lepage *Ring*. There were cast members who likewise added their voices of discontent to the proceedings. It was presented again, and this time to weak box office figures—something supposedly quite unprecedented in the history of the *Ring* at the Met. Some voices of the opera world were now moved to cite the Lepage *Ring* as the sign of everything wrong with the Met, and indeed the world in general. The Met moved on. Six years passed. Initial reactions ebbed. A new cast was assembled—one that seemed to have a different point of view on the production in general. The notorious machine was rewired, quieted down, and otherwise reengineered. It was time to bring this *Ring* production back and have a new experience of it.

I was ready. As a radio commentator at the Met, I am always ready for Wagner in general and the *Ring* in particular. I had written about it over the years, done dozens of talks about various aspects of the work in many different cities, and I never once had to scratch my head wondering what new things I could say about it. So even though the *Ring* adds a ton of extra work to any opera company vainglorious enough to take it on, from the ushers to the wigmakers, from the bartenders in the house to (not least) the musicians, and even to the radio commentators, I was looking forward to the three cycles being presented that season.

The Met needed the talks I proposed, in my opinion, because every opera company I ever encountered had them. Los Angeles had them, and

Chicago. I myself had given them on one occasion in Washington, DC and twice in San Francisco. Speight Jenkins, the legendary general manager of the Seattle Opera from 1983 to 2014, gave talks before AND after every *Ring* performance there. Even Wagner's own self-celebrating festival at Bayreuth had them, invariably given by some impossibly erudite German professor of Wagnerology (or whatever they call it) to audiences trying to project an air of comprehension about the subject that is invariably indigestible even for those who have mastered the German language and its pesky dative adjectives.

It didn't matter what was said so much as that it was being said, and that the company was providing this sort of "concierge experience" (in modern marketing parlance) for people who had spent a lot of money and invested a lot of time in attending this all-consuming work. The notion of having a talk (let's not call it a "lecture" for now, with that word's daunting intellectualism and its associated feelings of panic) provided a welcome to the audience, a reassurance that attending these performances was—after all—a good idea. In the case of Speight Jenkins in particular, the effect was very much of someone's friendly uncle telling you about all the fun things waiting for you in the wonderland—given by a sort of Wagnerian Willy Wonka.

What was needed was a bridge—a rainbow bridge, to shamelessly steal one of Wagner's images—from the quotidian world *out there* into the mystical space (Wagner's term, and a good one) in the theater. He knew that the transition between those two worlds was challenging and unnatural. That's why he wanted to build his Festival House to begin with, and to be built in such an out of the way place (then as now) as the provincial town of Bayreuth. You had to go, as a pilgrimage (which, of course, it entirely was and remains), to *a place apart* from the daily grind. He foresaw the difficulties of appreciating this work for the person who would be running from the office across town, hoping to make the necessarily early curtain for these operas, perhaps wolfing down a *Bratwurst* (readily available at the Festival then as now) to allay the dread of facing long acts on an empty stomach, which is precisely the only way most of us in New York and other places that are not summer festival destinations ever experience the *Ring*. Furthermore, the insouciance of providing no welcome whatsoever simply wouldn't suffice for audiences anymore. It probably never was a good idea to strike the pose of being the "Greatest Opera House in the World that is selling The Greatest Theater Piece Ever Composed (at premium prices) and you peasants in the streets should fork over your money and a week of your lives and just show up and love it, and if you don't, you must be terribly stupid," but it was clear that such a pose—or even the possibility of the appearance of one—was unsustainable by 2019. Wouldn't some welcoming chats, ideally in the lobby of the Met, be a good way to start countering that perception?

The Met's management was disturbingly enthusiastic about my proposal; I don't think I was fully prepared for it to green-light my idea. The first reaction was that this would be something we could offer donors, the people who had given money specifically to remounting the *Ring* and who needed to be thanked. Well, I countered, were the donors the population most in need of these talks? And wouldn't the donors already know the many resources available, from the Opera Guild to local music schools, for further study of this work? Management agreed. They then suggested we bill these as aimed toward newcomers, first timers to the *Ring*. Well, I countered, were newcomers really the population most in need of these talks, since they would already have so much information, from program notes to website features to ads for opportunities for further study, to digest? Management agreed. So the question became: "At whom are we aiming these talks?" The obvious answer came to all of us simultaneously: "At everyone." It had to be so. Everyone had to be targeted: the newcomer to opera; the operagoer new to Wagner; the bedraggled spouse going along for the ride; the Wagner fan who had never attended a performance of a *Ring* opera; the one who had never attended a complete *Ring*; the ones who had been once years ago but weren't quite sure what they had seen; the super-veteran who had been to every *Ring* production from Manaus to Bangkok; the academic who would know far more about the subject than I would (why deny it?); the Know-It-ALLS from the laity who attend every lecture that might even possibly contain the proper noun "Wagner" with the intent to root out (and point out) any error on the lecturer's part (and there is always at least one of these present); the moralist who finds this subject to be the root of all the world's evils and who intends to ask the lecturer pointedly what he or she intends to do about rectifying the sins unleashed by this Pandaemonium of art; the modernists and futurists and populists seeking relevance in the *Ring* as the source of everything huge and hip and now, from Tolkien to *Thor* to *Game of Thrones*; and the Guardians of Culture for whom the *Ring* embodies all the edifying glories that can be attained by means of *Kunst*. Every one of these people had to be borne in mind in preparing something to say. It wasn't a matter of who "needed" to be addressed, but what sort of a framing of the *Ring* experience could benefit all these people.

Then there were logistics.

The lobby of the Met was impossible to use. The union people in charge said it would require squadrons of workers to set up chairs, rope off the area, direct other traffic, set up sound, and everything else. One of the first practical lessons of the *Ring* is that you must never piss off the workers who are trying to accommodate you, so farewell to the dazzling marble Met lobby! This represented a dent in my vision. I really wanted this to happen in that exact physical space between *out there* and *in here*. But it was not possible. We would have to do them in List Hall—the exact place where I did not want to do it.

Most veteran opera fans can spend decades going to the Met and never know what or where List Hall is. List Hall is a small auditorium on the south side of the Metropolitan Opera House, on the same level as the orchestra seating, more or less. It seats 200 people in a steeply raked floor plan of about twenty unbroken rows (in other words, a modification of the Wagnerian notion of the ideal theater). The Opera Quiz is produced live there on some Saturday matinee broadcasts, with audience members attending during intermissions. I remember listening to the Opera Quiz when I was much younger, hearing Peter Allen announce, "And now coming to you from List Hall" and wondering if that was some remote venue somewhere down in the West 30s. I also was never quite sure whether it was "List" Hall (and if so, to what list did it refer?) or "Liszt" Hall (and if so, why would an opera house pay tribute to that wonderful composer and figure of the music world, but notably unoperatic, Franz Liszt except maybe, just maybe, because he was Wagner's father-in-law?). I write and produce the Opera Quiz now, and I spend a lot of time in List

Hall. It is also where the chorus spends some of its rehearsal time, and occasionally there are some truly interesting presentations given there (e.g. contemporary composers unpacking their works for attentive audiences).

It is also the ugliest room in the world. It is not even magnificently ugly, like the Belmont Room two floors up on the Grand Tier level with its silken moiré wallpaper in a disturbing green-tinged shade found only there and in one or two decayed Park Avenue morning rooms. No, List Hall is where operatic visions go to die, with all the charm of a suburban library's all-purpose room. The bare walls of List Hall are covered with beige burlap curtains (they were probably white when the building was new in 1966), its red velvet seats have faded unevenly like a scab, and the two staircases on either side of the seats are deliberately uneven, inevitably sending at least one wobbly dowager tumbling ass-over-tiara to the bare space below which serves as a sort of undivided stage area. But List Hall was where I would have to be.

The space having been determined, I needed to figure out the issue of time.

I was told I had twenty minutes to address people before each of the performances. I said I needed thirty. (I needed ninety but I figured I would commence bargaining with thirty). I was told I could have twenty-five. As it turned out, they all went about thirty-five, which in retrospect was an acceptable if not downright miraculous compromise.

So what the hell does one say in about half an hour before each of the four operas that comprise the *Ring*? What information do people need in order to pass from real life out there into the theater where the *Ring* is presented? Seen within those criteria, the question becomes one of what people do *not* need. What should I *not* say? The temptation to which many people succumb—including (and especially) those who are supremely well informed—is to take an opportunity to talk about the *Ring* to show how much he or she knows about it or indeed about anything, since the *Ring* is, or can be made to be, part of any erudite discourse. Whether it's music history, music theory, theater history, scenic design, literature, mythology, psychology, architecture, philosophy, and, perhaps above all, politics, you will come across the *Ring* in the course of your inquiries if you have a deep interest in virtually any subject. And any of these can be very, very interesting. But the problem for my purposes was that those tangents carry the subject from having experienced the *Ring* back to the world rather than getting people from the world to the *Ring*. My goal, I figured out, was to inspire interest in the audience members for this unique work. And the interest I would inspire (or augment, since they needed to have some level of interest already to have come this far in the journey) would be one that would open their portals of wonder in an engaged and focused manner for the entire long work. All I had to do was to light that spark. Wagner himself, diabolical wizard that he was, would take care of the rest.

That meant I had to throw away a lot of my "greatest hits." I wouldn't be able to talk about the various ways of producing Wagner on stage, and ways to interpret those productions. I wouldn't be able to give the topic of Wagnerism leading up to and during the Third Reich the attention and detail the subject requires in order to be addressed responsibly, but neither could I gloss over it. So I decided to address it from the angle of what we were doing right there in the audience—that is, interpreting the *Ring* for ourselves in a new way, which has the potential go horribly wrong ... as it did in the Third Reich. And there were other subjects, too, that had to be trimmed according to our immediate needs. Having rather inexplicably spent twelve years working in architecture and design, I was positively teeming with interesting information about the role of Wagnerism in those fields. But all that, too, would have to find another means of egress from my turbulent head. I wouldn't be able to talk about the plot, because enough, already, with the plot of the *Ring*. It's written in the program, online, everywhere. It's not *that* difficult. I write scripts for Met broadcasts and have to summarize very complex plots in two or so minutes. The *Ring* operas are surprisingly easy—although the shorter you make them, the more they lend themselves to comic interpretations (as the monologist Anna Russell brilliantly revealed in the 1950s). Incidentally, the supreme bitch of operatic synopses is Mozart and Da Ponte's *The Marriage of Figaro*. The *Ring* is entirely straightforward by comparison. So, no need to "take up time" reviewing the plot. And the most glaring omission from my talks would be that classic stand-by of

Wagner lectures: the dreaded analysis of the leitmotifs (the system of musical themes that identify people, things, and ideas throughout this work). There wasn't time for leitmotif deconstruction, and that can easily become more of a diversion than a tool to unpack the experience.

I decided my priorities were as follows:

- *How* to listen, rather than *what* to listen for;
- Addressing the *Ring* as an organic, evolving work of live theater rather than as a monument that was delivered perfect and complete from Wagner-heaven, like some sort of artistic Qu'ran, that has only degraded since the Edenic moment of its premiere in 1876;
- Cleaving to the idea that all commentary on the *Ring*—including mine—is ephemeral, and understanding that every production of the *Ring* is, in a sense, elaborate commentary on the piece. What is true in one moment may not be true in another. It probably isn't true in another place, and even if it is, it cannot be true in the same way.

While I can say here that the plot of the *Ring* is relatively simple, it can be unpacked *ad infinitum*, with implications and ramifications and structures that bear lifetimes of discussion. It is superficially simple, but vast. How, then, is one to view this plot? Same with the leitmotifs. Even I, with my two-fingered pianistic abilities, can sit at a keyboard and wow an audience by demonstrating, for instance, that the theme of Wotan's spear (representing law and culture) is an obvious inversion of the Rhine River (representing—you guessed it—nature). That's easy. But the subject is vast—far, far beyond the time allotted to me. There is truly no limit to how many discoveries can be made just looking at where Wagner placed the damned notes on the musical staff. So instead of enumerating the hundred or so leitmotifs, I decided to prioritize the angle of *how* they functioned, and why that was important. And the same with politics. What Hitler said about the *Ring* is one thing, and far beyond my abilities to address in a responsible way at this point. *How* Hitler found things to say about it was within my scope and imperative to address for this audience. And so forth…

I realized that a large part of my job as a commentator was to erase much of the previous commentary on this subject—or, if not to erase, then to set it in a contextual perspective. That's how it is with the classics. You have to talk about the talk.

Previous commentaries weren't bad or wrong. Okay, some clearly were. Wagner's granddaughter Friedelind (whose sister Verena, incidentally, died during the presentation of these talks in the spring of 2019, demonstrating again that much of this subject was less "way back then" than people might assume) wrote of sitting in the Bayreuth Festival House and eyeing the very top brass of the Nazi Party, amazed that they didn't see that this drama was about them—and not in good ways. So, some interpretations of this widely subjective work are just flat-out wrong, but most are not. Previous commentaries were just expanding on what they saw in their own time and place. It is we who are wrong if we cling to perceptions that may no longer be true to us simply because of the intellectual force with which they were originally stated. It doesn't make us as smart as them. It only makes us as dead as them.

Think about Virgil's *Aeneid*. It was praised to the point of literary deification when it first appeared, and largely because it apotheosized the divine mission of Imperial Rome. Well, you and I don't care about the divine mission of Imperial Rome other than historically, if at all, and in fact the very idea seems vaguely or actively toxic. So, do we dispense with the *Aeneid*? Many have – as this book goes to print Oxford University is considering removing it, along with Homer's *Iliad*, from required reading lists for Classics students -- but I think that is an error. The *Aeneid* is vital and eternal, but just not for the reasons that Augustus Caesar thought it was. It is the commentary about the work that we have to move aside, or rather, to reconsider within context as commentary, not the work itself. And we have to make sure that we do not confuse the two.

All the commentary that has been written on the *Ring* (from Nietzsche to George Bernard Shaw to Gertrude Foster Brown and the many other leaders of the women's movement of the early twentieth century who were passionate Wagner devotees, to Jung, to the ideologues of the Third Reich, to Theodor Adorno, to Susan Sontag and beyond) and every production of the *Ring* (from Wagner's own in 1876 to his wife

Cosima's to Heinz Tietjen's in the 1930s to Wieland Wagner's in the 1950s to Patrice Chéreau's in 1976 to Harry Kupfer's in the 1980s to Otto Schenk's at the Met in the 1980s and 1990s to Francesca Zambello's in Washington and San Francisco in the 2000s and 2010s to Robert Lepage's now) were evolutionary steps in our understanding of the *Ring* today. They were not, however, definitions of how we *must* understand the *Ring*.

To cleave to someone else's interpretation is to dedicate oneself to things that no longer exist, and in aiming to gain the virtues of those who first stated these visions, we become grotesque simulacra of them. This is what happens to several characters in the *Ring*. This is, in fact, what the *Ring* is actually about, and we will see that our relationship with this core quality of the work becomes the single most amazing aspect of it. We, too, as well as those characters, either evolve, or are destroyed in one way or another by the course of its evolution.

The Retro Theory

When it came time to start getting rid of deadweight commentary about the *Ring*, I found one notion in particular that was long overdue to be tossed overboard. There has been a prevailing narrative that the reason this massive work turned out as it did is because Wagner wrote it backwards, beginning with the last part, *Götterdämmerung*, and finishing with the first part, the so-called "prelude," *Das Rheingold*. There is just enough truth in this supposition to be truly misleading. Indeed, Wagner did conceive of the entire grand drama in reverse. First came the idea for a very large scale pseudo-historical epic opera based mostly on the medieval German epic poem *Nibelungenlied* which he originally titled *Siegfrieds Tod*, or *Siegfried's Death*. He then became interested in exploring the roots and motivations for this drama, and conceived a prequel (as we now say) called *Der junge Siegfried*, or *The Young Siegfried*, beginning the exploration of Norse sources for information about the enigmatic title hero that was not to be found in the *Nibelungenlied*. The process continued with Wagner exploring yet more sources, and then supplying additional "information" from his own famously turgid imagination to fill in what he felt was missing from that janky narrative until he had the four dramas as we know them.

This retroactive composition, according to that prevailing narrative that I wanted to jettison, is the reason there are so many supposed repetitions in the *Ring*—the retelling of stories that we already know since we saw them unfold on the stage one or two nights previously. That's why there are so many "boring" monologues and "recaps" in this work, says this point of view. Those Norns at the beginning of *Götterdämmerung* that so many people complain about, or think they are supposed to complain about, tell a version of everything that has gone before. Wotan does the same thing on several rather lengthy occasions. And so forth.

This understanding of the composition of the *Ring* can be misleading because the reverse composition only holds true for the prose outline of the work—a detailed outline, to be sure, but only an outline nonetheless. Most of the actual words, the libretto, and all of the score were written forwards, from beginning (*Das Rheingold*) to end (*Götterdämmerung*). And in any case, he had twenty-eight years to work on the damned piece and certainly plenty of opportunity to notice where he might have had cause to say "oops, I guess I already said that."

The Retro Theory persists and has powerful champions. No less an exalted personage than George Bernard Shaw emphasized it (although he knew the actual facts of the composition as well as anyone) in order to illustrate his Great Point about the *Ring* in his commentary, *The Perfect Wagnerite* (1898). Shaw was both a socialist and a music critic, and his most intense interest lay in the intersection of these two passions. How the musical and dramatic structures expressed analogous political structures was, to him, the most important and interesting aspect of the *Ring*. Seeing the *Ring* through a lens of a socio-political music history timeline revealed many insights, even if Shaw necessarily bent both the *Ring* and history in order to torque them into something that would illustrate his point.

According to Shaw, the beginning of the *Ring* (that is, the first part conceived, and therefore the end as we know it, *Götterdämmerung*) was written (if not actually composed) in an earlier world, by a less mature artist than the last part of the *Ring* (which is to say, the beginning as we know it, *Das Rheingold*). World history and Wagnerian biography both bear this out to some extent. The prose sketch of *Siegfrieds Tod* was complete by 1847. Socialist Shaw, naturally, was the last person in the world to underestimate the effects of the Revolutions of 1848, which changed the face of Europe (and beyond), bringing such names as Marx and Garibaldi (among many others) to the world's attention. Wagner himself was caught up in the general conflagration, siding with the revolutionaries (and even the leftist fringe of them as represented by his sometime companion in Dresden, the Russian anarchist Bakunin), and was exiled from the German states for his troubles. By the time he finished conceiving the *Ring*, Europe changed. So did Wagner: the exile read political and transcendental philosophy, ran up debts, found himself well outside the musical establishment of his day, and began to realize he needed a new method of expressing his genius. The old forms typical of opera (especially the Italian and French operas that he claimed to detest) would simply not be able to function for the radical ideas (and music) he now needed to share with us mortals.

Shaw and his acolytes saw an analogy between traditional forms of opera on the one hand and traditional forms of government on the other. Put another way, the notion of opera as a formulaic system of set pieces (arias, duets, trios, choruses, and combinations thereof) separated by recitatives (those "talky" parts in between the "big numbers") seemed positively reactionary by the mid-nineteenth century. The goal for progressive composers of the time was the seamless, "through-composed" work, in which there was no clear delineation of form (aria, chorus, et al.), if those forms could be identified at all. It had formerly been that all the action took place in the recitative, and then aria (or other set piece) reflected on the action that had just happened. The "recits" (as the pros call them) convey information, the set pieces unpack characters' reactions to said information. Therefore, recits tend to be, by design, based on speech patterns or a heightened version of them, while the set pieces tended to be a chance for melody and the singers' virtuosity to gush forth and dazzle everybody. Wagner and the other progressives, then, were inclined to admire the recits as the brainier parts, and to look down on the set pieces as mere crowd-pleasers. The astute modern reader will recognize many analogues from our contemporary music scene in any genre, from new classical to Satan-worshiping death metal: incomprensibility must perforce indicate depth while any catchy tune must perforce lack merit.

But of course there is an obvious problem: recits get old fast, and people actually like melody. Wagner himself, perhaps ironically, could spew out hummable tunes with the best of them ("Here Comes the Bride," or "*Treulich geführt*," the Bridal Chorus from *Lohengrin*, circa 1850, the mass popularity of which annoyed Wagner in his own lifetime). His solution to the "recits over there, big hits over there" problem was to understand the whole piece as endless melody (a term especially applied to his 1865 brain-frying musical masterpiece *Tristan und Isolde*) and the entire libretto as both a conveyance of information and a response to that information, kind of like in actual life as he understood it. Whether or not Wagner was entirely correct in his contempt for the old forms, there can be no denying what he achieved with his new way of looking at things.

Nor was he alone in his attempt to find a more holistic approach to the idea of "music drama" (he was among the first to make the word "opera"—meaning traditional opera before he rescued it and turned it into something better—a bit of a dirty word, which is a sense it still holds today). Wagner's contemporary Giuseppe Verdi (they were born in the same year) was on the exact same trajectory down on the southern European side of things, even if he was characteristically a bit more polite toward his artistic ancestors than the ever-ornery Wagner (who, even in his operas, must always have a "bad guy" to be excoriated—and he was even more vicious in real life). Verdi, too, worked hard to move from the recit-aria-recit-ensemble-chorus pattern of his earlier, undeniably thrilling operas (*Nabucco*, 1842; *Ernani*, 1844) to a more integrated structure in which it often became difficult to say exactly where the recit ended and the set piece began (such as in *Don Carlos*, 1867, or the revised *Simon Boccanegra*, 1881). Think of his final masterpiece, *Falstaff*—a gem of lyrical-dramatic unity that would have made even the already-dead Wagner gag with envy. Clearly, the best musical minds of the late nineteenth century were on the same wavelength, even if they barely acknowledged each other.

The late nineteenth century, however, was a long time ago. It wasn't only a long time ago chronologically: it was a long time ago in the history of time itself. Wagner and Verdi lived time differently than we do. Every generation has perceived time differently for a while now. George

Frederick Handel (1685–1759) was one of the geniuses who made opera popular beyond Italy, and his works helped solidify the recit-aria formal construction for a century. After his lifetime, his many operas disappeared. No one thought they would ever resurface, and they have only done so in recent decades.

What changed wasn't the quality of the brilliant music or even the tastes of the audience. Certainly, the style of singing necessary to make the music sparkle had vanished with the disappearance of the *castrati* (a whole subject of its own), but that is still an insufficient explanation: audiences tolerated and cherished Handel's vocal music in the oratorios and other religious music. The change was in the public's understanding of time. In Handel's day, time was reckoned by people as they needed to reckon it in the spot where they were. A sundial was sufficient for most purposes (canonical hours, for example), and lunchtime happened when the guy whose job it was to ring the bell decided either that the sun was in mid-sky or that he was hungry. By some mechanism, that being-in-the-moment, closer-to-the-earth-and-its-cycles world had no trouble accepting that some moments in time were for the consumption of information (like recits) and some moments in time were for that information's digestion, reflection, and elaboration (like arias with their slow and fast sections).

Industrialization changed everything. Linear time needed to be invented and accepted by wide groups of people: factories needed to start and stop assembly lines on given schedules; children who now lived outside of the earshot of bells needed to get to school on time; and, most famously, trains needed to run according to a communal timetable—a lesson learned by bad trial and worse error. The suddenly ubiquitous bourgeoisie thrived on linear time and linear thinking, which had its analogous literary expression in the oft-noted rise of the prose novel during this same era. Those things, whether material or artistic creations, that moved from A to Z were modern, and those that did not were (quite literally) out of step with the times at best and probably reactionary. Audiences and critics alike considered Handel's operas absolutely out of the question.

Interestingly, his oratorios were highly, even maniacally, popular during this time, especially that perennial juggernaut of all oratorios,

Messiah. That's because sacred time is experienced differently than secular time. The goal of all meditative practice is in fact to remove one from linear time. So that which is old-fashioned in everyday life becomes possible and even essential when one is being self-consciously spiritual. Just look at television commercials at Christmastime: fuzzy images of wooly, candle-lit family gatherings that would be laughable or abhorrent during the summer become *de rigueur* during the holidays. Similarly, audiences could permit themselves to savor the time-suspended glories of Handel's vocal music at the edifying sacred choral concerts so dear to Victorian hearts, while laughing at the absurdity of those same glories at the opera house. Think of the finale of *Messiah*: four minutes of repetition on the single word "Amen"—and one of the most sublime things ever created.

So while Verdi and Wagner and their contemporaries were obsessed with "not stopping the action," that ideal did not represent a manifesto of how all music should forever be (no matter how much Wagner might have said it was), but rather a goal for how they needed to compose in order to best express the artistic notions of their own time. In fact, in an odd way, they created immortal works by being perfectly attuned to their own moment in time. (This happens everywhere: filmmakers talk about how a movie made for its own moment, say *Casablanca* or *2001: A Space Odyssey*, will last forever, while one made with the ideal of being in some sense portentous and eternal like, say, *Heaven's Gate*, will soon be forgotten). What Wagner called "The Music of the Future" was in fact "The Music of Right Then and There." And that was its greatness.

Let's return to Shaw. As a man of his time, he too was keenly interested in a structural critique of music and was equally obsessed with it even if he saw its limits. He famously suggested that the reason Wagner and Verdi had become so interested in creating through-composed operas like *Tristan* and *Falstaff* was because they had each in their old age run out of youthful great tunes like Wagner's "Ode to the Morning Star" (*Tannhäuser*, 1845) and Verdi's "Il balen" (*Il trovatore*, 1853). The suggestion, of course, is that a good tune is hormonally driven, while a brainier construction is something of interest primarily to older men of diminished lust. But while Shaw saw the absurdity in Wagner's theorizing (as he saw the joke in everything, including his own genius), he still subscribed to the notion that through-composing was somehow right and set pieces connected by recits were somehow contemptible. Remembering the "Retro-Composition Theory of The *Ring*," this meant for Shaw that *Götterdämmerung* was "mere" grand opera (written before Wagner and the world "grew up" in 1848) while *Das Rheingold* was non-commercial theoretical music drama of the highest order, with the second and third parts of the *Ring*, *Die Walküre* and *Siegfried*, being somewhere in between. For Shaw, this meant that the entire *Ring* was a long, drawn-out disappointment, a descent from something new and exciting to another thing as distressingly banal as Grand Opera with all its excesses and cheap effects (which Wagner himself had condemned in language much plainer than one reads here).

Was Shaw wrong? Shaw was a genius, obviously, so how could he be so flat out wrong? (A good question we will be asking about Wagner quite frequently in the upcoming pages). The answer is that Shaw was right to deconstruct the work in front of him the way he did when he did, and we can learn a lot from reading him. We should and we must read Shaw and all the other great commentaries on the *Ring* (Newman, Adorno, et al.), but—and here is the whole issue right here—we must read them not as definitions (literally, boundaries, endpoints) of the *Ring* but rather as evolutionary steps in our constantly growing appreciation of it. This is not 1896, and our concerns are not Shaw's or anyone else's but our own. For one thing, we do not inhabit time in the same way people did in 1896. Linear time is old-fashioned. Einstein came along in 1905 and began his process of articulating Relativity. Richard Strauss unleashed his opera *Salome* the same year (not, I think, a coincidence—or if it is, it's a hell of a one). Pablo Picasso's time-and-space-bending painting *Les Demoiselles d'Avignon* came along in 1907. All of a sudden, for whatever reason (cosmic shift in world consciousness, market forces … who knows) the best minds understood that some moments in time took longer than others. Or perhaps they remembered what industrialized life had temporarily distracted them from, since Handel knew that perfectly well when he composed the *Messiah* "Amen." And lo and behold—science fiction suddenly came along to make time travel an essential component of every gasp-inducing film narrative. "Flashbacks" are common everywhere from Proust (who wrote a seven-volume novel touched off by one memory revived by a tea biscuit) to psychedelia. This is the sensibility that we all grew up with. We don't care that a narrative goes from A to Z in order to be up-to-date, and we shouldn't pretend we do just because so many people wrote about that so well. It's all old-fashioned now. Live theater is old-fashioned, so there's no use talking about whether Wagner or Donizetti is more the music of the future.

We don't need to repeat what erudite people said a hundred years ago: it doesn't make us erudite. In fact, it's intellectually lazy. And Shaw, for one, would have made terrific fun of us for doing it.

The "Marketing Approach"

There is another structurally flawed way of unpacking this vast work that also makes it a great disappointment, and it is also one begun by Wagner himself and carried out to the present day. I call it the "Marketing Approach," although it began before the word "marketing" was in use. It involves identifying captivating musical segments (a more cynical person would say "sure-fire hits") and then flogging the public with them at concerts and elsewhere (including films, commercials, cartoons, and everywhere else in our modern era), and then hyping the *Ring* as a motherlode of such tunes. In other words, play the big hits at the public whenever you can to create some interest and then let everyone trudge through the "boring parts" in between. This was done by Wagner and his admirers in the two decades before he finally managed to stage the full *Ring*, and it is hard to see how he could have avoided doing so. Of course when you have such great two–to–six minute tunes as "The Ride of the Valkyries" and "Siegfried's Funeral Music," why would you not? Well, a lot of reasons. Because even though the motivation behind this impulse to "play the hits" appears to be the diametric opposite of "praising the through-composed, non-flashy unity" impulse, the net result is identical. It makes the *Ring* boring (cf. Anna Russell's succinct introduction of the character Wotan: "and he's a crashing bore"). A full 90% of the *Ring* is two people talking to one another (I counted over the course of one indolent summer). If you attend a live performance because, like every other sentient being, you found "The Ride of the Valkyries" exciting, there is no way you can be anything but stultified by the other fourteen hours of it. Conversely, a desire to savor the full depths of the *Ring* can also be frustrated by hearing it in snippets, as many of Wagner's contemporaries opined.

A Third Way

Both of these approaches—the intellectual method stressing the new forms of the work and the emotional approach hoping to grab the listener with boffo tunes—were so far from my own experience of the work that I knew there had to be another way to serve it up to an audience. For one thing, my own experience of the *Ring*—of sitting through it and experiencing it live in the theater—was that it was a work of absolutely perfect coherence. When I got to the last notes of *Götterdämmerung*, I had this distinct feeling that it had been heading there the whole time. And every preceding moment was bringing it there. This is something one rarely feels in an opera house, or anywhere else for that matter. One can almost always detect the composer "picking at the piano" in some sense, wondering, "Where should I go next? How do I bring it all home? I wonder how it would sound if I wrote *this* now…?" Some works even make that sense of disjointed contrast their own exalted art form—I'm thinking of the genius art of Mahler symphonies, which revel in this atmosphere of "Oooh look… a funeral march! No wait—now there are children playing! And bells ringing … Bing Bong! Aww but now everyone dies again …," and so forth. Again, I am not saying there is only way to compose. But I remain blown away the undeniable feeling of the impressive coherence in this longest singe piece of music ever composed (or at least, of any music that has been heard more than once or twice). Wagner knew where it was going the entire time—the music says so undeniably. And I often say in talks—partly for shock effect, but mostly because I actually believe it— that there are only two operas ever composed that can be said to have not one single unnecessary note of music, and they are Puccini's *La bohème* and *The Ring of the Nibelung*.

You may be able to stomach that statement, or you may not. What is important for an audience's purposes is to consider what I have learned from being able to say that, which is something quite contrary to what they will glean from Shaw or from leitmotif memorization or from greatest hits repetitions, and that is this: What if Wagner meant for the *Ring* to be exactly as it is? What if everything is exactly in the order he intended, for the reasons he intended, and as long as he intended?

When I posed this question to myself, the whole tetralogy became a bigger experience for me as both a unity and as four discrete operas. And something occurred to me that could not have occurred to commentators of the nineteenth century: if the *Ring* is a perfect unity, and the result was intentional, then Wagner must have intended each of the four operas to be a little different in how it tells a story. Each opera represents a different stage in the evolution of the world, and one tells stories differently in different worlds: one way when the world is new, and another when the world has a past. The "pure-theory music drama" world of *Das Rheingold* so beloved of Shaw and others is not brainier—it is simply more appropriate to the world of gods and magical creatures it portrays. The "Grand Opera" sensibility of *Götterdämmerung* is not a reversion to an older set of norms, as even such great twentieth century commentators as Ernest Newman and George Martin thought, but rather what some deride as "mere" Grand Opera is the better way to depict the world of humanity with its politics and its messy emotions.

When you look at the *Ring* like this, every single moment of it becomes vital and necessary, and every single moment of it is there for a reason. There are no boring parts. When Wotan (or Siegfried, or the Norns) tells the "whole story again from the top," it becomes different each time. It becomes a story about storytelling. And I find that very interesting. And that's how I decided to talk about the *Ring*.

It won't do anymore to present the *Ring* as a bunch of spectacular moments interspersed with dramatically flawed boring parts. People won't put up with this any longer—and not just because people have shorter attention spans. It's because the *Ring* is much better than that, and audiences have evolved to the point where they have figured that out.

Chapter II
About *Das Rheingold* ...

Confusion exists between all the interesting aspects of the *Ring* that form a lifetime of—I don't want to say study, exactly, but ... unpacking, exegesis, on the one hand, and what information we actually need to experience a live performance of it on the other. The great singer Eileen Farrell (who never actually sang Wagner at the Met, but that's another story) wrote in her autobiography that a neighbor of hers in Staten Island once said, "Oh I don't like Wagner." Farrell said bluntly in return "That's because you don't know how to listen to him." To her credit, Farrell then sat down at her record player or her piano, I forget which, and painstakingly explained to her neighbor how she understood Wagner to work, emphasizing the system of leitmotifs spread across the *Ring* and how to hear them. This is not what I would have done with that dismissive neighbor, but it is similar to the manner in which I would have fielded such a question if I had been so inclined to bother. What I think Farrell got right was identifying the problem of misunderstanding or failing to grasp Wagner as an issue of how one listens to it. When I proposed these welcome talks—let's call them—my intention was to provide a sort of bridge from the real world to the magic of the opera house, and I realized what would best serve everyone is context.

I'll share a quick story. There was a woman who worked in the Metropolitan Opera's press department who had been involved with the punk scene in London in the 1970s—as I was, too, though only a little, to be honest (I'm actually from Los Angeles), but I had spent just enough time in that London scene as a teenager to be able to follow her stories. And one day she and I were here attending the final dress rehearsal of Handel's opera, *Giulio Cesare in Egitto.* At the end of it, she was walking up the aisle with that glazed-over look on her face you can get after a really good few hours on "planet Handel," and she said in spacey voice, "I get it … it's just like punk."

Now, if you know Handel's operas, you might admit that there are a lot of ways one could think to describe them before settling on that correlation. They are heavily reliant on strict forms. There were 43 or so "set numbers," of which all except two or three were solo arias, each connected by harpsichord-accompanied recits. This is not the sort of thing that inevitably conjures images of Sid Vicious puking on the audience. So I raised an eyebrow and pointed my palms upward in a gesture that said "care to explain that?".

"I mean it." She went on. "Because without context, it really is just noise."

I had a genuine revelation.

It is always my job to give context, and that is the entire extent of my job as a commentator. But there are a lot of different ways to do that. The context I want to give now is inspired by Eileen Farrell – it is in the *how*, rather than the *what*. As a memorable character in another composer's opera, the Marschallin in Richard Strauss's *Der Rosenkavalier*, says, everyone's going to get old and die—but it's in the *how* that lies all the difference. The *what* is virtually infinite, if we think of the *what* in our present case as background information on Wagner and the *Ring*. There is more written on Wagner than any other secular person, with the possible exceptions of Napoleon and Winston Churchill. That is a quantifiable fact. I have myself contributed to this deluge of Wagnerian sludge but I do want you to delve into that sludge. We can't jump into it here but we can explore ways of broadening the immense experience of the *Ring*—ways of looking at it that augment the experience for newcomers and veterans alike … a wide bridge … a Rainbow Bridge for all, one could say.

If you are engaging the *Ring* for the first time, then you are about to take a journey unlike any other in the arts—one that encompasses (although you may not realize it all at once) music, drama, stagecraft, the visual arts, psychology, politics, history, mythology, cosmography, and—quite possibly—everything else. And you're in a perfect position to appreciate it all. A hundred years ago, the common wisdom was that Wagner was "advanced" opera, and you should take newcomers to "easy" operas like Puccini's *La bohème* or Donizetti's *Lucia di Lammermoor*. I doubt that was ever really true, but I know it is untrue today. I've had great luck bringing people to Wagner for their first opera. You get what he's telling you by the time he's done telling it to you. I talk to a lot of different groups, from kids to retirees, and I have to spend very little time explaining the mechanics of Wagner's music. I do, however, spend a lot of time explaining melody to audiences today. A hundred years ago, people in Europe and the Americas were immersed in the idea of one correct way to make music. Nowadays Donizetti's use of melody, for example, confuses people. Why do characters sing so prettily when they're about to do something awful? The use of melody in Donizetti, to show a level of commitment of the character without regard to whether the action in question is "pretty" or not, confuses us today. But Wagner, by contrast, is "easy."

Live performance is how the *Ring* was designed to be experienced—and it is weird but (I think) undeniably true that it seems much shorter sitting in the theater than listening to recordings or even watching taped performances of it. In fact, it is exactly the right length, but I'll get to that.

Veterans—or "Ringheads" as they are sometimes known—embark on a journey as epic as the newcomer's, because one thing we learn from the *Ring* is that hearing the same story at a different time in your life—and in the life of the world—makes it an entirely new and different story. But I'll get to that, too.

Sixty years ago, common wisdom dictated hours of homework at the piano or the record player in order to get through a live performance of the *Ring*—among other reasons, there just weren't that many live performances of the complete *Ring* right around then, and no full-length recording existed until the early 1960s. A hundred years ago, the emphasis was on written commentary. But again, that is additional to—not necessary for—experiencing a live performance.

There are also other paths of advice, and they can be equally untrue and in fact quite distracting. There are many people who will tell you to ignore all the extraneous ramifications of the *Ring* – the political issues above all – and instead to focus on enjoying the great music. I will not argue with the greatness of the music. It has never been surpassed. But I would not suggest you come here just for the incredible music because, for one thing, that is not possible. Music, as our punk friend pointed out, can only exist in context or it is nothing but organized noise. The politics cannot and should not be dismembered from any work, least of all this one. But there's a more practical reason not to come here just for the beautiful music: you can hear great music at much less inconvenience, and—why deny it?—expense. Music is basically free nowadays—even this music, which is all over YouTube. There must be a bigger, better reason to attend a live performance of the *Ring*.

The reason to come here is for truth.

Now please wrap your heads around this: the truth you get from experiencing the *Ring* in a live performance is not literal. Far from it. Wagner was wrong about almost everything he said in a literal sense. He was wrong about the Jews being the cause of the degeneration of music. He was wrong about miscegenation causing the degeneration of humanity. And he was wrong about meat-eating causing the degeneration of public morals (although he himself was not, as is commonly believed, a vegetarian). Also, somewhere else in his two dozen volumes of turgid prose he probably says the exact opposite of everything he's already stated. Case in point: Judaism. After a lifetime of excoriating the Jews, he says in his final essay "Know Thyself" that the Jews are "probably the noblest race of all." Now even if there were any truth to be gleaned in such a blanket racial statement, it, too, would be wrong just by existing in the context of Wagnerian bloviation. So even when he says his own opposite, he somehow manages to be, yet again, wrong.

So, let's dispense with a search for literal truth in Wagner or any other artistic masterpiece. Yet there is a deeper truth to be had in the *Ring*, and uniquely in the *Ring*. This work has its roots in Norse mythology and medieval German legend—or rather in Wagner's reading (and, more importantly, *mis*reading) of them. However, it also has roots in Greek and

Roman mythology. The all-important format of the *Ring* is modeled on the ancient drama festivals of Athens: a prologue of sorts and three tragedies all experienced by the entire community as a quasi-religious spectacle in the course of a very long day. It was in fact this classical provenance that most excited Wagner's one-time worshipful acolyte (and later arch nemesis) Friedrich Nietzsche, who wrote about it at length in his essay *The Birth of Tragedy* and who in many ways set the parameters for all future discussion of the *Ring*. One classical work that I think is patent in the *Ring* and that I find helps me to understand the *Ring*'s structure, meaning, and grandeur is Ovid's *Metamorphoses*. The first lines of that poem read: "I want to speak about bodies changed into new forms. You, gods, since you are the ones who alter these, and all other things, inspire my attempt, and spin out a continuous thread of words, from the world's first origins to my own time."

The classical world did not differentiate between word and music the way the modern mind does—and neither did Wagner differentiate between the two the way most modern people do. Wagner, like all great opera composers but surely second to none, uses music neither as a salve nor as a distraction but as a means to tell his story. And by story, I don't mean plot. Forget the plot for now. I mean story, as in Logos. The truth that I think one finds most authentically at the opera—at any opera, really, but most supremely in this supreme work—is an insight into the nature of transformation: how one thing becomes another thing. And by "thing," I mean everything:

- the growth of a thought or feeling
- how love becomes hate
- how a person becomes a monster
- how insistence on our rights and our property becomes criminal to the point of fratricide [cf. *Genesis*, Remus and Romulus, John Lennon: "but first you must learn how to smile as you kill... if you want to live like the folks on the hill... a working class hero {cf. Fafner and Fasolt} is something to be ..."]
- how one political order becomes another

- how a pantheon of gods dies in modernity
- how an entire world order becomes another world order

… and so on.

All this, as Ovid said, is the story of everything: cycles of birth, life, decline, death, and rebirth (and all birth is rebirth, said the great Ovid scholar Norman O. Brown, which may explain how a birth and a rebirth can resemble each other … and yet be different). That is the real reason why we refer to the *Ring* as a "cycle." It's not just a term of convenience for the box office (although that, too). It is because the work is about cyclical reality. This is precisely what Wagner does so well in the *Ring*. He sings about bodies and things changed and changing from the world's first origins (at the very beginning of *Das Rheingold*) to our own times (even beyond his own), to the time of humanity after the era of the gods, glimpsed at the end of *Götterdämmerung*, in one single continuous thread. I promise you that if you stay with this epic through the end, you will see as I have seen that you were heading there the whole time, from the first note of *Das Rheingold* (183 bars of E flat spun out in all its ramifications) to the conclusion of *Götterdämmerung* (D flat chord: one step, one note, down from where we started); it is one continuous thread. Wagner must have had it all—all the dots, all the notes—in his head at one moment like a super dense star about to supernova and explode a plethora of elements across the universe that reform to become new worlds, which is in fact exactly what the *Ring* itself is.

So if we agree to be schooled by our Straussian friend the Marschallin—our "mama from another drama"—how do we approach our audience roles as not so much nouns or verbs or even adjectives, but as adverbs? How do we *how*?

I wasn't going to give advice, but I'll advise this: Think big and listen hard. Assimilate all the information—both in the theater and all the contextual information—in this way.

Now, a word about these leitmotifs everyone talks about …

These are musical themes associated with people, places, actions, and (above all) ideas, deployed systematically throughout this epic and providing a sort of architectural frame allowing such an immense work to stand coherently. Wagner did not invent leitmotifs, nor did he even give them this name (he used the term *hauptmotif*), but no one else ever used them so elaborately or effectively. I confess that I spent twenty years telling audiences that leitmotifs didn't matter anymore and that people shouldn't worry about them. My rationale was that since Wagner's time we have learned to live in a world of leitmotifs, in movie soundtracks and advertising jingles and elsewhere, and therefore we didn't need to study them the way people were told to a hundred years ago. But now I think that approach was essentially wrong. We certainly don't need to study them in the way people did a hundred years ago, but I think we benefit from looking closely at them in ways that are appropriate to us and to what we know. Leitmotifs are ideas, and we now have a great word for multiple aspects of ideas: intersectionality. Let's apply it here.

The psychological aspects of the *Ring* that may have intrigued Carl Jung might have been most apparent at moments like you will experience in the first of the four scenes of *Das Rheingold*, in which the character of Alberich the dwarf commits an epochal act of sublimation when he transfers his lust for love (or whatever one would call it) to a lust for gold. Then the political allegory aspects that fired up George Bernard Shaw, for example, might be most apparent when Fricka is arguing with Wotan, while another interested commentator—say, the suffragist and Wagner lecturer Gertrude Foster Brown would have had different takeaways from that very same scene. The real glory of Wagner's art—the truth of it, since it morphs from one thing to another with Ovidian fleetness—lies, however, in combining these aspects into one holistic vision. What matters is how all these different things look and sound and feel and exist in relation to each other, in each other's contexts. The result prefigures Werner Heisenberg's uncertainty principle, the great brain-fry of the twentieth century: that observing something actually changes that thing. It does: it makes it a different thing. So, therefore, different people observing or considering something must also turn that thing into different things. Observing or otherwise interacting with it at different points in time likewise turns it into yet something else. It is the ever-evolving intersectionality of ideas, and Wagner's mastery of it, that makes the *Ring* unique.

You can hear this in the finale to tonight's opera, *Das Rheingold*. It's like all the themes we have heard up until that point (and parts of themes, and variations of those themes), are layered one on top of the other—yet the result is a single, very grand piece of music that is sometimes heard out of context and therefore with much less substance in the concert hall and elsewhere (including movie soundtracks). What matters, however, is not how much we hear but that we hear and somehow feel the themes in relation to each other. Each strand of music becomes infinite by the prismatic virtue of Heisenberg's multiple point of view equations. This is the moment at which the orchestra, I am told by people who would know, is the loudest in all of the *Ring*—right there, at the finale of *Das Rheingold*, including seven harps here at the Met (the covered pit at the Bayreuth Festival House in Germany requires twelve). Why does it need to be so very loud? It's not just because it's a good time to make the most noise for a gangbuster grand finale. Wagner takes the exact opposite approach with the finales to *Die Walküre* and indeed to the whole cycle at the end of *Götterdämmerung*. It's because there is truly that much going on in conflict with everything else, and what matters is how those goings-on relate to each other. A very similar thing will happen during the orchestral prelude to Act III of *Siegfried*—one of my favorite moments in the whole *Ring*—where conflicting characters are about to face off at the literal crossroad of destiny. (That moment is also the chronological crux of the whole cycle, coming at about halfway through it if you time the music without intermissions from beginning to end.)

In the movie π (Not *Life of Pi*, but just π), there was one thing that really struck me. A math genius is about to complete the sequence of numbers that make up all the decimal points in the irrational number Pi, which everyone always thought was infinite. It also turns out to be the numerical identity of God. Everyone is trying to get the number out of him, from the stock market to religious sects, and one group—the Hasidics, I think—capture him and tie him to a chair and slap him around trying to get the number. He yells at them something to the effect of "The numbers are just numbers. It's the spaces in between them, and their relationship to each other... THAT'S God!"

I had another genuine revelation, because I realized that was the way to observe ... well, everything, really ... but opera above all. I realized that the themes, even when we give them a fancy name such as leitmotifs, and even when they're awesomely memorable, are just groups of dots on a page, and what matters is how the space between them makes them interact with each other. And this "mystical space" (to use Wagner's term for theater) is accessible to the *Gestalt* mind as well as to the incrementally analytical mind—rather more so, in fact. I especially don't think it's necessary to diagram and otherwise flow-chart the leitmotifs in *Das Rheingold* because it is in *Das Rheingold* that the leitmotifs get their meaning. We usually see the thing (person, place, action, or idea) to which the music is referring when we first hear that music. It is in the subsequent operas that the music will recall—and often as through a glass darkly—the issues that were plainly set forth in *Das Rheingold*. That, as much as conformity to any Athenian ideals of format, is probably why this is considered a prologue to the *Ring*.

What I would ask anyone seeing the Cycle to do is watch and listen actively, in a way we usually don't with movie soundtracks and advertising jingles. Ask yourself what it really sounds like to you. Then ask if it sounds the way it did before. Has it changed? Why is it making me think of that other bit of music? Trust your gut, but make sure you engage your gut. Because if your gut is engaged along with your eyes and ears, then it doesn't matter so much if you could answer on a pop quiz that you know Wotan's spear with its runes of law is the River Rhine in reverse: culture is the mirror image (and opposite but parallel reality) of nature. The relation isn't perfectly symmetrical in any case. Nothing in the natural world in—neither the earth nor the planetary orbits are the perfect circles the ancients wished them to be. The relations are as relative and as bumpy as the humans who describe them.

You can study this score for a lifetime—and I hope you do, along with all the other theory and exegesis coming out of it, from Nietzsche to Theodor Adorno, to Jung, to Frank Lloyd Wright, to Susan Sontag, to Tolkien (a lot to talk about there), to George Lucas, to George Bernard Shaw, to Gertrude Foster Brown, to everyone else. But you don't NEED to memorize the leitmotifs (or anything else said about the *Ring*) in order to take this journey. You just have to listen actively, trust your gut about what you are hearing, and remove the limits your mind places on the possibilities of what you are experiencing. Because there really is no limit to it; it is that big.

I was talking once with the soprano Christine Goerke about singing the role of Brünnhilde, and she said "There is no one who has sung this who hasn't had a core relationship with it for the rest of their lives." I realized it was the same with me as an audience member regarding the entire piece, and it will be the same for anyone.

Chapter III
About *Die Walküre...*

As pilgrims on the Road to Santiago say to each other as they cross paths over several days, "Buen camino"—because that is very much what's going as we arrive at the second installment of *The Ring of the Nibelung*: *Die Walküre*, or *The Valkyrie*.

Die Walküre, a continuation of *Das Rheingold*, is the next logical step in this journey, and an entirely different planet—all at the same time. So, what is it? How is it like the rest of the *Ring*, and how is it quite unlike it? First of all, it is the most approachable of the *Ring* operas. If you have seen only one *Ring* opera live, chances are pretty good it was this one, and it is often staged on its own.

The vector of the *Ring* is from the ethereal world of the previous age to the world of today, where humanity (for all its faults and its more-pedestrian-than-the-gods nature) is at the center of the universe, and giants and dwarfs and dragons, if they exist at all, are remote and unreal. Therefore, *Das Rheingold* is going to present information in one way, *Die Walküre* and *Siegfried* (which have a lot in common, structurally) in another transitional way, and finally *Götterdämmerung* in an entirely different way. The *Ring* only becomes more and more "operatic" because it is more "human" (read, messy), just as *Das Rheingold* is more "cerebral" because it is more "ethereal" (literally, of the ether, the light air that the gods breathe). One can find hints to the varying dimensions of each individual opera in the libretto itself. For example, one of the very first things Wotan said last night in *Das Rheingold* was a chronological brain-fry: "*Vollendet das ewige Werk*," or "The endless work is finished." It's even backwards syntactically to make it even more complicated: "Ended is the eternal work."

That. Makes. No. Sense. Or does it? Picasso's game-changing painting *Les Demoiselles d'Avignon* (1907) can be viewed as just bad draftsmanship—you can't have an ear on someone's face over there somewhere and a nose or two way over there on the other side—until you understand that multiple moments of time exist in the same moment. The bodies are in motion, or seem to be, because of the traumatized state of the observer who is confronted with such raw sexuality. Hyperaware moments are outside of linear time. It's clear then that the painting is not only brilliant draftsmanship but also a masterpiece of internal psychology, and universal physics as well. Applying a spirit of "intentionality" to Wagner's creation of the *Ring*, let's ask this: what if he meant to pen a line as "stupid" as "*Vollendet das ewige Werk?*" Might he not be telling us that *Das Rheingold* exists in a dimension where time does not work the way it does in *Götterdämmerung*, much less in our world? It must, or else Wagner is just very stupid—and that seems unlikely, whatever else he was.

What happens in *Die Walküre*—and I don't mean who does what to whom, although there is plenty of that to discuss, but rather, what really happens—is that we leave the above and below worlds of *Das Rheingold* (the bottom of a river, the mountain peaks around Valhalla, and the caverns of the dwarfs) and dwell on the earth, the realm of humans... you and me. There were no humans in *Das Rheingold*. There were idealized humans (gods) and then there were grotesque, humanoid analogues (dwarfs, giants, *et al.*). But *Die Walküre* is in the next phase of the world—the time is not even specified in general terms, as it will be (interestingly) from here on. We can deduce that there has been enough time for Wotan to have fathered children on the earth and seen them grow to young adulthood, but we don't know how long it took him from having the idea to do so (at the very end of *Das Rheingold*, when we read in the stage directions that he is "struck by an idea" and then hear a theme in the orchestra which we will only find out tonight has something to do with a sword and these children) to committing the necessary deed with an unnamed human woman. In any case, the world of people is still very, very young. We are in the First Age or something close to it, as science fiction writers would call it today. Phenomena that are strictly human are rather new, coarse, and still in formation: tribal structures, social relations, and—

above all—emotions. The idealized humanoids, the gods, interact with real humans with explosive results. Each side (gods and humans) is transformed by the encounter. The grotesque humanoids, we are told, are asleep or otherwise engaged offstage throughout this opera.

To tell this story, Wagner uses some of the tools of conventional opera—lightly, to be sure, and not as overtly as he did in *Götterdämmerung*. And commentators a hundred years or so ago—I'm thinking of George Bernard Shaw and Ernest Newman—would have fought me over saying he did anything conventional in this work. Yet we will find this to be true from our perspective. In Act I, Siegmund sings the "Spring Song." Newman spent pages telling us why this is not an aria, like in some bel canto opera. The "Spring Song" may not be an aria like those in a bel canto opera, but it is an aria nonetheless. So is his sister/lover's solo *"Der Männer Sippe"* that follows. Wagner not only uses form similarly to how others used it, but he also uses melody in ways he hadn't in *Das Rheingold*. We hear great melody in "The Ride of the Valkyries" at the beginning of Act III, but we must prepare ourselves for the gut-ripping, tear-jerking, emotion-based melody during "Wotan's Farewell" at the end of that act.

Shaw and Newman liked to think of the "retro theory" of the *Ring*'s composition because it helped them to understand it as Wagner's journey. Wagner, according to this approach, matured from a great opera composer in 1847 to a revolutionary artistic thinker by 1852, and thus the *Ring* traced that journey in reverse from Revolutionary Theoretical Abstract Art back to Really Great Opera. This was a step down for them. But if we use my "Wagner Meant to Do It This Way" model, which I think has the additional advantage of being true, then we see material not even those great lovers of Wagner could see. And some of it is quite mind-blowing.

For one thing, if we stop seeing bel canto and Italian contemporary opera as things to be shunned, then we can see how great those works are in their own way—which is not after all so very different from Wagner's work. I believe time has corroborated this point of view. The long-lived notion that Wagner was smart and Italian composers were just *tuney* and emotional but not very brainy is tired at best, and legacy racism at worst.

That's why I don't bother with the music drama appellation. You're at the opera. Deal with it. In fact, one way of looking at Shaw's and Newman's insights is to see the *Ring* as one glorious journey from dry philosophy into magnificent, wonderful opera. The *Ring* justifies, rather than kills off, opera itself.

But there's more. Among the new creations we encounter in *Die Walküre* is the most deceptive aspect of the human experience, memory. Not only do Siegmund and Sieglinde struggle to recover lost memories in Act I, but Fricka also spends time reminding Wotan what he said in Act II, and Wotan will do the same to Brünnhilde in Act III. Most notoriously, Wotan spends an inordinate amount of time rehashing what happened to him (or how he remembers things happening to him) to Brünnhilde in Act II—and even she is shocked by these revelations, or more accurately she is shocked by the very fact that Wotan is revealing them. Apparently, this sort of "sit down and let me tell you a story" was entirely unprecedented in this world and quite unthinkable for Wotan himself. Again, Newman took great pains in 1940 to explain to us that Wotan's monologue was in no way like that which one finds in that arch-demon of all Italian operas, Verdi's *Il trovatore*. That opera begins with the guard captain Ferrando telling a "once upon a time" spooky story. Actually, Wotan's monologue is exactly the same as that—it's just a different way of doing the same thing.

You tell a story one way when the world is new and another way when the world you're depicting is strained under the weight of its own history. And this is something I think Wagner and his contemporaries would have felt very keenly. What, they must have asked themselves, do we do with all this damned heritage we're always told we should appreciate? What about that Holy Roman Empire, the First Reich, which only passed away in 1806, and that Roman Catholic Church that Wagner's father-in-law Liszt became a part of, and those castles that lie in ruins and need to be reimagined by the contemporary Romantic imagination (like Schloss Neuschwanstein, designed by the court opera designer, no less, and loving decorated with Wagnerian imagery)? The twelfth-century epic poem *Das Nibelungenlied* has a much different way of telling this story than the nineteenth-century *Der Ring des Nibelungen*. And so *Die Walküre* requires a different language, or way of delivering language, than *Das Rheingold*, because a significant amount of time has passed and the world is a different place. The leitmotifs take on symbolic meaning they didn't have in *Das Rheingold* because they were not yet recalling (symbolizing) anything. The "Curse on the Ring" theme was a literal curse on the ring, not a reference to the curse on the ring.

Actual language itself is not so different. I had the opportunity to study Sanskrit a few years back, and I learned that one of the notions of that language is that it is the pure, perfect language of the gods, and that all other languages are devolutions of it. Inherent in that conceit was the idea that word and meaning were one and the same in Sanskrit—the word somehow contained the actual essence of the thing it described rather than being a referent to it. Of course I thought that was a bunch of hooey. Then one day I was working with my vocabulary flashcards—on the subway, I think—and I was in the group of animals, and I saw that the word for owl was "gookhaha." And I said it aloud. Gookhaha. I thought wow, that really is the right word for an owl… certainly better than "owl." In fact, the thing in question IS a gookhaha. And I realized maybe the Sanskritists were on to something after all, even if it cannot be called factual linguistic history.

Mid twentieth-century professors of semiotics had a lot to say about the notion that modern life was a study in the distance between the thing that refers and the thing being referred to. All meaning has been removed from actual experience and become referential, symbolic, "virtual." We've already seen some of that journey in the *Ring* and will continue to. What are the gods, for example? A deity is one thing when they're talking to each other in real and urgent situations, and quite another in symbolic reference (modern life). Note how Fricka changes between *Rheingold* and *Walküre*. She slept quite literally on the earth in *Rheingold*. In *Walküre* she will sit on a throne that is a chariot drawn by rams, per Wagner's libretto. She is in the process of becoming more of an idea than an actual living being. The process continues until, in *Götterdämmerung*, she actually (again per Wagner's libretto, and also well depicted in Lepage's production) is nothing more than a statue, an altar. She becomes, over time, a monument to an idea.

The great mezzo-soprano Joyce DiDonato explained something to me about baroque opera that also taught me a lot about Wagner. In baroque opera (Handel and others) the dominant form of an aria is A/B/A. That is, a singer sings the first chunk (whether a verse or other poetic unit), there is a central bridge section in which, most likely, the character will question (usually internally) what he or she had said in the A section, and then repeat the first section as a sort of resolution. That final section, then, will be ornamented more elaborately than it had been in its first iteration—grace notes and addenda and sometimes entirely new (and invariably florid) passages inserted. Joyce told me that the urge to ornament needs to be handled judiciously. Most people, she thought, overdid it, functioning too much on the theory that Handel wouldn't have wanted you to repeat the same thing you just heard. But here was the important thing she told me regarding Handel that schooled me on Wagner: The music cannot be the same as what you already heard, precisely because you have already heard it. It is by definition a different thing. And not only that, but the singer is different—the actual voice is different—for having sung it once. Similarly, you in the audience, your ears, are different from what they had been because you had already heard it once. Behold the great discovery of every pop song, bad and good, in creation. You can repeat the exact same thing and it will not be the exact same thing. And so even if Fricka, or any other character, sings the same notes tonight that she or he sang last night, they are not the same notes. They have been informed by time. Their meaning has been changed by context. They have been warped, if you will, by memory. (Note to those who will misquote Joyce DiDonato out of context: She did not say one should not ornament the second A section. She said one should not ornament it solely on the theory that failing to ornament would be to repeat the exact same thing, which is the reason usually given for ornamenting. Joyce is one of the great "ornamenters" of history—possibly because she has questioned the received wisdom of why she should do it in the first place).

We have entered the world of memory, and a lot of things come along with the centrality of memory that hadn't existed before communal memory was an issue. One thing that comes along with memory is melody, and I've already mentioned that we'll be wallowing in more of that tonight.

And another by-product of memory is religion. It simply doesn't exist in the Golden Age. It didn't in Ovid's Golden Age, nor in *Das Rheingold*, nor even in *Genesis* until Adam and Eve get tossed out of Eden and Cain and Abel have to offer sacrifices. According to Dante, there are no Church rituals in Hell, and there aren't any in Heaven, either. You don't need them in the latter and they wouldn't do any good in the former. There's only a Church pageant in Purgatory, which is the only realm that exists on the surface of the earth, and therefore in linear time. We are on the surface of the earth for the rest of the *Ring*, and in Act II of *Walküre* we will see Brünnhilde intoning the Annunciation of Death like an antiphonal psalm. It's clearly a religious ritual. Social conventions and religion are companions, and tonight will be the first mention of honor. Hunding speaks of it and abides by it. The concept didn't yet exist in *Das Rheingold* and will become corrupt to the point of meaninglessness by *Götterdämmerung*.

I think the most central issue we face with the addition of memory is the whole world of storytelling and everything that goes along with that: legend, myth, and more. The memories and the monologues and the rehashings of the plot will continue right through to the very end of the cycle (Siegfried's recovering of memory triggers his own death in Act III of *Götterdämmerung*, and Brünnhilde's comprehension of all that had happened before triggers the death of just about everything directly after that). In fact, the First Age is crushed by the weight of its own past. This, actually, is the story of the *Ring*.

It's also our story attending the *Ring*. We can either be crushed—overwhelmed—by the weight of everything that has been said about the *Ring* and done in its name, or we can use all that as a springboard toward personal and critical evolution. What do I mean?

Every production of the *Ring* is a form of commentary on this great work. It stresses what one person wants us to see in it. Some are more eloquent or memorable than others, but none is definitive. And all commentary, as I keep saying, is best considered an evolutionary step in our communal understanding of the piece rather than a summation of it meant to last for all times.

Wagner spent decades not only finishing the *Ring* but also trying to find the right way to present it on the stage. He finally had to have an entire new theater built according to his specifications, at national budget-breaking expense, to mount it, getting the very best designers and collaborators to put on the best possible, even ideal, production. This happened in 1876 in Bayreuth—and at the end of it, he and everyone had a vague sense of disappointment in the production ("The Ride of the Valkyries," for example, having been a huge letdown ... not due to any failure of vision or execution but merely because one cannot make perfectly seen that which cannot be seen). And he said, "Next year we'll do it all differently." Only there was no next year. The national budget failed to finance the next year's *Ring*. Wagner got busy on *Parsifal*, and he died in 1883 without ever restaging the *Ring*. But while he never told us how he would restage it, he told us something very important when he said he wanted to. He reminded us that the *Ring* was a living, breathing, growing, and (yes) dying organism. It was not a monument to a living organism—not a stone statue, much less a fossil. Of course, that is exactly what it became for many people after his death—especially to his wife, Cosima, who saw her role as the guardian of the legacy more than a creator of a new one. But I'll tell you the best reason to think of the *Ring* as something ever-renewable: If you don't, you will become embittered. If you do, you will be empowered.

Indulge me with a detour to the sources of the *Ring* for a moment. Ragnarok, or properly, Ragnarøkkr tells the Old Norse myth of the end of the age of the gods, a great final battle in which they and almost everything and everyone else dies and is reborn from a few surviving humans and from the earth. It means "Twilight of the Gods," and the German for this is, of course, *Götterdämmerung*. We know that *Götterdämmerung*, under Wagner's original name of *Siegfrieds Tod*, or *Siegfried's Death*, was the ever-expanding kernel out of which the *Ring* was born. This *Ring* we're dealing with is an amalgamation of several sources: mostly one large German epic poem, the *Nibelungenlied*, and also several different collections of Norse mythology. Those sources contain some of the same characters, or various versions of those characters, but are very different from each other in theme, tone, and incident. *Götterdämmerung* derives mostly from the *Nibelungenlied*, except in one very important way, and then the farther back you go into the story (meaning the first three operas), the more the work derives from the Norse sources. The important way in which *Götterdämmerung* and the *Nibelungenlied* differ is that there is no end of the gods in the *Nibelungenlied*. So whatever else the *Ring* is a journey toward, it was clearly made to be (at some narrative exertion on Wagner's part), a road to Ragnarok.

I had cause to mention Heisenberg's Uncertainty Principle earlier—the effect of observation on the observed—and must do it again. I don't know if Heisenberg said anything about the effect of observation on the observer, but I do know that Christine Goerke thought of that when she said her encounter with Brünnhilde changed her as a performer.

The mutual Heisenbergism we find in the musicalized world of opera is that a performer leaves a stamp on the role but the role leaves a stamp on the performer as well. And in *Walküre*, we will see in remarkable ways that characters leave a stamp on, and essentially change, each other as well. In the Act II encounter between Siegmund and his (unbeknownst to him) half-sister Brünnhilde, in that "Annunciation of Death" scene, Wagner practically underlines it in neon lights with some deft chord and key changes telling us that we (like Siegmund) are suddenly in contact with a new dimension. A portal has opened. And the mortal Siegmund will defy the Valkyrie Brünnhilde by telling her he must obey a stronger command than hers, one dictated by love.

The most significant character-transformation-by-encounter-with-another-character happens at the end, however, during "Wotan's Farewell." It's one of the most fascinating (not to mention devastating) depictions of a power exchange anywhere—and a disempowerment exchange, an impotence exchange. You are assumed to know the outcome of the *Ring* before it happens (remember Ragnarok? Everything dies). In *Walküre* Wotan feels compelled to remove Brünnhilde's divinity as a punishment for her disobedience. He explains that she has actually removed her own divinity by exercising a will contrary to his godly one and by siding with human love over divine decree. And he accomplishes this metamorphosis with a kiss. But kisses work both ways, and indeed it is not only Brünnhilde who is changed on an existential level by that kiss, but Wotan as well. When we look at it in retrospect the next time we meet him in *Siegfried*, he won't even be the King of the Gods anymore, but a ghostly simulacrum of what he had once been, the half-hidden-by-a-slouchy-hat Wanderer. But we already hear the transformation in *Walküre*, in plaintive music that is full of pain, severed ties of love, and remorseful. The libretto tells us that tonight Wotan is turning Brünnhilde human, but the music tells us that tonight he is turning himself human.

In both cases, the supposedly greater creatures have become infected by a supposed weakness of the supposedly lesser creatures, love. It reminds me a bit of H. G. Wells and *The War of the Worlds*, in which the supposedly invincible Invaders from Outer Space are killed off, not by the strength of the warrior earthlings, but by the earthlings' smallest companions, our germs. I believe it's the common cold that fells the indomitable space aliens. "What do you get when you fall in love? You get enough germs to catch pneumonia."

None of this would be of any urgent interest in our limited time except that it leads us to the most astounding aspect of this reciprocity, this post-Heisenbergian observer/observed interaction, which is the effect it has on each of us. I remember what I learned from our friend the Marschallin in Richard Strauss's and Hugo von Hofmannsthal's opera *Der Rosenkavalier*, that it was in that *how* that lay all the difference. ("*Und in dem 'Wie' da liegt der ganze Unterschied.*")

In fact, the Marschallin's *how* is also Ragnarok. The gods are going to lose the final struggle. Everybody knows this. Wotan himself will say so in that much-maligned and misunderstood Act II monologue tonight when he cries out *"Das Ende!"* as what he wants most. But this does not devolve into mere nihilism, because the Norse thought it was very, very important how you conducted yourself toward and in the final battle of Ragnarok. And it wasn't about securing your place in the Afterlife with good conduct because this already was the Afterlife—you had to die well first just to be worthy to die forever on the last day! (This is something we hear strange allusions to when Brünnhilde tries to announce Siegmund's death to him as something he should feel excited about, in Act II). And yet the *how* on the road to oblivion was held to be all-important.

For years I thought Ragnarok was rather ridiculous—or at least was an insufferably grim Nordic notion that had little to do with my rather sunny, mostly Mediterranean-derived disposition. I was also suspicious of nations that killed off their own gods. Then the Marschallin taught me that the myth of Ragnarok was about each of us in everyday life. Why do laundry? You will just have to do it all over again. Why shave, or even eat? What's the point? It solves nothing, and you'll grow old (if you're lucky) and die anyway. But just maybe, if you do it with a certain intentionality or a certain presence in the banalities of daily life, you can become something admirable and memorable, as she did. She even concludes that time itself, even with all the ravages it inflicts on our beauty and our hopes and dreams, must be a good thing, since it, too, "is a creation of the Father, who created us all." (*"Auch sie ist ein Geschöpf des Vaters, der uns alle erschaffen hat"*)—a line that might have popped fully formed out of the libretto of *Die Walküre*.

That is the real story of Ragnarok, and that is the real story of *Götterdämmerung*, which is the real story of the *Ring*. And the Marschallin's application of it to everyday life (and death) shows us another way that it's a cycle. If we apply Christine Goerke's observation to ourselves, reverse Heisenberg-like, then we can see the *Ring* as one big challenge to ourselves. Will you become an embittered Bayreuth originalist who insists that the 1876 production and the original Hans von Wolzogen commentary on it are sacrosanct and inviolate? Many do. You'll see some of these people at intermission, ready to pounce on you as you try to get a cup of coffee or a sandwich if you show any sign of having—GASP—enjoyed a new production, which is of course WRONG because they'll tell you that this production sucks (which is odd to hear them say, because I am now old enough to remember the very same people, or people who looked and sounded a lot like them, saying the same sorts of awful things about previous productions), and that this conductor sucks (same thing, from the same people), and that the Brünnhilde sucks compared to Birgit Nilsson in the 1960s or Kirsten Flagstad in the 1930s or Olive Fremstad in the teens or Lilli Lehmann in the 1890s, depending on how orthodox and crystallized they wish to be. Wolzogen himself became the darling of the most pernicious Wagnerians, the racist proto-

Nazi reactionaries of Bayreuth and beyond. Is that what you want to be? Or will you take the more challenging but more rewarding path of embracing the evolutionary essence of this work, and see in new productions and new commentaries and new performances nothing more and nothing less than different points of view giving a greater and deeper overall sense of this piece that can and should never be entirely comprehended? What is your *how*?

In other words, will you become Alberich, forever holding on to that one thing that happened in the past ("I swore off love and forged the ring and it was stolen from me … whaaa whaaa whaaa!") or will you become Brünnhilde, and see that you might have to throw away something that is most "precious" (à la Tolkien) in order to cleanse it and keep yourself and everything else moving forward? Which means that each and every one of you must decide how you will tread this path—as Alberich, or as Brünnhilde, and choose to be destroyed or renewed. You will grow old and die anyway, someday if not soon. In a sense it doesn't matter—and yet it does. *Der Rosenkavalier. Ragnarok. Götterdämmerung.* You're a part of it. Which means, if you think about it, that when we experience the *Ring*, we are actually living its true story—its logos.

All of this means (if you really think about it) that Wagner has both anticipated everything Heisenberg taught us about cause and effect but also proven in it in action, with the world audience as the subjects of the experiment. This, it seems to me, is a consideration of absolutely psychedelic proportions.

Chapter IV
About *Siegfried...*

Now we come to part three of the *Ring's* four installments, *Siegfried*. This is considered the "scary" one of the four, the "most difficult." Sometimes subscribers get spooked from what they have heard about *Siegfried* and give their tickets away. Anna Russell, in her comic monologue about the *Ring*, said, "There isn't much you need to know about this opera." She then goes on about it hilariously for several minutes, both acknowledging and undercutting the general prejudice. But I brought my friend Sandy to *Siegfried*—and only *Siegfried*—in San Francisco last summer. It was her first Wagner opera. And of course she loved it, or I wouldn't be referencing it now. She said to me afterwards, regarding all the warnings and the faux concerns people expressed about her attending a performance of *Siegfried*, "What was everyone freaking out about?" I have to say that one of the reasons it is not as scary as people thought seventy years ago (Anna Russell's routine is now about seventy years old—can you believe that?) is that simultaneous translations, such as Met Titles, have made it a much more approachable work. Of course you must not keep your nose in the Met Titles, and of course you should read the libretto ahead of time (and good luck making sense out of reading a Wagner libretto without the music), and of course you should study German and understand every word or pretend you do like audiences did during the imagined Golden Age of pre-dumbed down modernity. Let's face it: translations have actually helped many operas, and perhaps none more than *Siegfried*.

Often there is always that one guy—and it is always a guy, somehow—who will say that *Siegfried* is his favorite of the four operas. I am that guy. Yup. And I am not alone. Erich Leinsdorf, who was one of the Met's most important conductors from the late 1930s right into the 1980s, once said something really striking. He said the three things that made being a conductor worthwhile were Beethoven's Ninth Symphony, Stravinsky's *Rite of Spring*, and *Siegfried*. I don't claim to know anything about conducting, but there's something about that statement I find perfectly credible.

To repeat my earlier observation about *Das Rheingold* and *Die Walküre*, there is an infinite amount of information we could not discuss. I suggested that leitmotifs were important, but that we need new ways of looking at them. I further argued that we could either experience the *Ring* as something to destroy ourselves in some sense or to renew ourselves, which was its true meaning (both the actual little ring that fits on a finger in the story and the whole operatic epic). I also suggested that if we look at the *Ring* not as a jerry-rigged monstrosity created haphazardly over almost three decades but rather as a vast work that came out exactly as its author intended it to (compare in your minds to Tolstoy's *War and Peace*), then we could find as many new veins of gold to mine as there are in Nibelheim. That means we should first look at how *Siegfried* is part of the chain that forms the *Ring*, and then look at how it is something of its own.

If we look at the entire *Ring* as a whole, we see that *Siegfried* and *Die Walküre* occupy similar central places, even though there is more time between them than between *Siegfried* and *Götterdämmerung*. Again, in a narrative sense as well as from our point of view as audience members, *Siegfried* and *Die Walküre* are in a sort of geographical if not perfectly chronological center. *Das Rheingold* is the realm of gods and magical creatures—how does that dwarf breathe underwater, anyway?—while *Götterdämmerung* is almost all mortals, except for brief visits from doomed Norns who disappear after admitting they no longer have any knowledge of events; a worried Valkyrie whose concerns fall on deaf ears; that same magical dwarf, who may merely be a character in a mortal's dream; and those pesky Rhine Maidens, who are as feckless as ever.

So *Siegfried* and *Die Walküre* are in the middle in an evolutionary sense as well, the epoch between the First (Golden, Edenic) Age and the Modern Age of Humanity. This middle time is the era when gods and magical creatures interact with humans. In fact, here they're all vying with each other to see who will be the rulers of the world, the Definers of the Era. In Greek mythology, this was the Age of Heroes—and it's important for us to remember that a "hero" in Greek mythology meant someone who was mixed human and divine, mortal in that he is subject to death, but descended in part from the gods, as are Hercules, Jason, Achilles and Agamemnon, as well as, of course, Siegfried. It was this Era of the In-Between (both in time and in essence), the Silver and Bronze ages, that gives us almost all of the Greek myths. In fact most of them refer to just a few generations, a mere blip in the timeline of humanity. This is also the mythologically fertile era that gave us opera itself, which began entirely committed to tales of Daphne and Orpheus and their friends and maintained such an influence over opera throughout the centuries. The Trojan War was the turning point. The myths all end a generation after the Trojan War. The gods stop interacting humans on all levels, and here we are … modern humans, dealing only with each other. The gods either died, as in the Norse Ragnarok, or they just stopped texting us for booty calls, according to the Greeks, growing distant and unavailable. They literally "ghosted" us. But that climactic moment of the Trojan War and its immediate, chaotic aftermath, left us with centuries—millennia—of the most evergreen myths. And it left us with many of the most memorable, and diverse, operas as well: *La Belle Hélène*, *Les Troyens*, *Idomeneo*, *Elektra*, *Iphigénie en Wherever*…. Opera as an art form is a direct descendant of the classical Athenian dramatists' reinterpretation of the myths from just before and just after the Trojan War, that provenance that so impressed Nietzsche in relation to Wagner in *The Birth of Tragedy* and elsewhere. And Freud and Jung turned to that same specific mythological era for archetypal models of psychological patterns as well. There's something fascinating and supremely important about transitional phases, about junctures and crossroads. The era of *Siegfried* and *Die Walküre* is a Northern European parallel. Siegmund and Sieglinde whom we met last night were half god, half mortal. So is their son, Siegfried, whom we finally meet in the flesh (as opposed to as a prophecy or as an embryo) in this opera. He is the next generation chronologically, but he has the same DNA as his twin parents. So in some sense they are all the same—transitional. Brünnhilde, as we saw at the end of last night's opera, managed this transition on her own, without any illicit spawning. She began the night as divine and ended it as human. Even Wotan has experienced a metamorphosis of sorts, or at least we humans perceive him as metamorphosed.

Let's remember the π formula: the numbers are just numbers. The spaces in between them and their relationship to each other are "where God lives," i.e., the important parts that give meaning (life) to the whole. One of the things we always talk about in opera, whether we realize it or not, is structure—how things are arranged. Whether we are talking about Handel, or Wagner, or Berg's *Lulu*, or anything else, we have to consider structure. And it becomes obvious that *Die Walküre* and *Siegfried* have very similar structures. Each has a first act with only three characters, and each first act is one complete arc from a restrained opening to a rushing finale. They're each single vast, if not perfectly even, crescendos. Both operas have a central second act in which all the "action" happens, each one being a chain of a half-dozen separate confrontations. Both operas have undeniably superb third acts, and both third acts end with extended and awesome duets.

There's more. Swords are important (both operas have the same sword, even if it is refashioned in *Siegfried*). Act I of *Die Walküre* ends with Siegmund brandishing his sword and declaring "*So blühe den Wälsungen blut!*" ("Let the Volsung [his and his sister/wife's, the children of Wälse, the name by which they know Wotan] blood flourish!" Act I of *Siegfried* ends with Siegfried brandishing his reforged sword and declaring "Look how sharp Siegfried's sword is!" ("*So schneidet Siegfrieds Schwert!*") in almost the exact same musical notes. Father and son are each demanding our acknowledgement of their respective virility as embodied in the archetypally symbolic sword. Siegmund will prove his mettle on Sieglinde immediately after his declaration; Siegfried will prove his on Brünnhilde a mere act and a half later. And Brünnhilde herself will acknowledge it in *Götterdämmerung*, when she lovingly claims to know the sword's "sharpness" (*Schärfe*) as well as its "sheath" (*Scheide*, a German euphemism for "vagina").

Both operas have extended passages of truly wrenching beauty. *Die Walküre* has its Act I duet and sob-inducing "Wotan's Farewell" to

Brünnhilde at the end, some of the most overtly emotional music Wagner ever wrote. *Siegfried* has its delicate Forest Murmurs, and its awakening scene for Brünnhilde in Act III – which may have been what Maestro Leinsdorf had in mind when he praised this score as career-justifying. The chords that accompany the sun hitting Brünnhilde's waking face, and the silences in between them, absolutely make my skin tingle, as we might imagine hers to do in that moment. They're also a real test of the orchestra's (and conductor's) abilities. The musical, dramatic, psychological, and thematic situation is also a sort of reverse parallel of the end of *Die Walküre*. There, Brünnhilde was being put to sleep, and sleep is the palliative antidote to the unbearable emotion of loss both she and Wotan are experiencing in that moment. *Siegfried's* finale is her awakening to new emotion, to love.

This parallelism (both direct and reverse) tells us something about form following function. Both operas occupy a nodal space of transition. It is a transition of form, in the earlier commentators' analysis, from Theoretical Music Drama to Grand Opera, with *Die Walküre* and *Siegfried* having elements of both. And we can see their function as taking us through a transitional era in the age of the world, in which characters have elements of the beings that went before and those that will come after (i.e., us).

So why is *Die Walküre* the most popular of the *Ring* operas and *Siegfried* saddled with the reputation of being the least popular? First off, it wasn't always so. After the 1876 cycle in Bayreuth and the next few, in Berlin and New York, it was the other way around. *Siegfried* was the most highly regarded of the four and *Die Walküre* was the most puzzling to critics and audiences. And this tells us that any understanding of *Siegfried* as a sort of problem stepchild must be a failure of contextualization. This all leads us to consider how *Siegfried* is different from the other *Ring* operas and what accounts for its differences.

One of the first things we notice when we encounter *Siegfried* is how few characters there are in it—shockingly few, for such a long opera, and still no chorus (that will come at long last in *Götterdämmerung*). And those few characters function very differently than characters elsewhere. How so?

Every commentary on the *Ring* tells us that Wagner put aside its actual composition (after completing the librettos and sketching copious notes for the music) while composing *Siegfried*, somewhere in Act II (there is some scholarly disagreement about exactly where). He put it aside for a long time—about twelve years. In the meantime, he composed and produced *Tristan und Isolde* and *Die Meistersinger von Nürnberg,* and then returned to the *Ring* with greater abilities as an orchestral composer. I find this asks more questions than it answers. For one, I don't think Wagner was lacking any powers as an orchestral composer up to this point, neither in the *Ring* nor certainly in *Tristan* or *Meistersinger.* I believe Wagner had to evolve to a place in which he was comfortable giving the orchestra a greater role as a sort of character of its own, because the orchestra changes in ways other than its composer's technical mastery over it toward the end of *Siegfried.* The history of the world demands a greater role of the orchestra after a certain point. It becomes more profound because more of what is happening on stage is happening as backstory and in the subconscious, which are inevitable by-products of the maturation of the world. The process of going deeper is apparent throughout this opera but I believe it became something Wagner needed to reconsider in a big way before he could finish it, and finish it with such magnificent mastery as Brünnhilde's awakening.

Not only is there more subconscious in the characters, there is more self-consciousness throughout this opera. Siegfried discovers fear. Brünnhilde discovers romantic love. Mime spends a lot of time wondering "what should I do?," although when he has a chance to ask advice from an expert, he fails miserably. Clearly, Mime has not evolved sufficiently in the course of self-consciousness to benefit from psychoanalysis. Wotan, who had just barely begun the process of questioning his own actions during his monologue in *Die Walküre,* now revels in self-evaluation, both in the third person when speaking to Mime, and more frankly when speaking to Erda. There is also much more weight of backstory because there *is* so much more backstory, and backstory is deceptive and murky and "down there" somewhere. The other characters exist as pure backstory: Fafner, Erda, and Alberich are entirely proscribed by that which occurred in the past. They have no further agency. The entire orchestral introduction to the opera is a dark slurry of memories afflicted by resentment and disappointment and thwarted ideals, and all the lies and hypocrisies that come with socialization and the advance of some form of civilization.

Along with these additional layers of backstory, we get more helpings of history. Not only are these supposedly repetitive monologues of Wotan and Mime in Act I and all the other retellings of what went before more inclusion of history in present situations, they make the opera as a whole more of a commentary on history itself. For example, we've had many opportunities to refer to Shaw's socialist analysis of the *Ring*, *The Perfect Wagnerite*. That worthy essay focuses heavily on this opera and its understanding of the character Siegfried as the proto-anarchist, a version of the real-life Russian Mikhail Bakunin, who had met and impressed Wagner in Dresden in the revolutionary events around 1848.

There is also in *Siegfried* rather a lot of time dedicated to forging a particular sword, a good half-hour spent going through the art of sword-smithing in preliterate Europe in what seems like real time. Why? Can this also be part of the historicity of *Siegfried*? Or is it merely just what the literalists will insist it is—a perfect example of Wagner's miserably long-winded dramaturgy meant to give vent to the tenor's powers of singing loud and hard? It cannot be only this, at least it cannot be so by accident. Wagner managed to depict the entire evolution of the world from the beginning of time to the invention of speech in just four minutes at the beginning of *Das Rheingold*. I can't believe he just "went on" at such great length about sword-smithing here because he couldn't think of any other way to make Act I the same length as Act III. So if we give Wagner credit for having intended this work to be what it is, what can we learn? Well, the first answer must be that he felt this whole sword thing to be very important, and that he wanted us to spend a lot more time than we usually do considering the significance of it within the context of the entire *Ring*.

Swords come from a later era of technology than spears, and Wotan's power, as we have seen, is represented by a spear. Swords represent a New Age: the Iron superseding the Bronze, (bronze swords existed, but they were rarer than iron swords and did not cause a revolution in warfare). For the Norse, swords were a great innovation, and specifically iron (and its even more effective alloy, steel) swords created from the quench-hardening technology that Wagner spends so much time going through in painstaking detail in Act I of *Siegfried*. This quench-hardening technology, involving plunging the still white-hot metal into cold water whose sudden cooling gave a mysterious hardness to the weapon, was unknown in Scandinavia until just before the Viking Age. In fact, it is this very technology that is credited as one of the innovations, along with overpopulation and major improvements in shipbuilding technology, that morphed the Norse tribes of legend into the warring, invading, globally known Viking nations of history.

Brian Eno once pointed out that wars are not fought between conflicting ideologies but between conflicting technologies (which may in turn dictate conflicting ideologies). I don't know if Eno originated that quote but that's where I heard it. Generations, then, are technologies in conflict, as any of us know who have had to do anything as banal as asking a younger relative for help using our iPhones. And generations are at war—either literally, as groups, or one-on-one, as in family conflicts, or even internally, in a Freudian sense, with Oedipal and Electra complexes and so forth. And all of these are present in the confrontation of sword-wielding young Siegfried and spear-wielding old Wanderer Wotan, who is not only Siegfried's grandfather but, genetically, his father, as well as a representative of a much earlier generation. The sword was originally planted by the father to be used by the son even if the father suspected (perhaps only dimly at first) that the sword would be used against him and make him impotent, fit only for death. But the sword is of no use to the son in the form in which the father bequeathed it. It went limp, became corrupt, useless. And even in its broken state, it needed to be smashed down further, into little bits, and then purified by fire, first, and then water (a process the entire world will have to endure in the subsequent opera) and put all back together by one who has a lot more brawn than brains. Youthful energy, rather than staid experience, is what's called for in this particular act of procreation. The youth in question even recognizes the unimportance of parental wisdom and the supremacy of his own rebellious power. He snaps at Mime in a manner typical of bratty, cocky youths snarking at representatives of their fathers' generation, "If I'd studied with you, I'd know even less!"

The oft-repeated (and easily parodied) "*Hei-ho!*" of Siegfried's Forging Song, which approximates the breathing sound of the bellows, is two notes up, and then repeated two notes back down. Those two upward notes are the beginning of the sword motif itself, which we first heard as "an idea" of Wotan's at the end of *Das Rheingold* and which can't have had any meaning to us in the audience (assuming we haven't read any commentaries) until it becomes explicitly associated with the sword in Act I of *Die Walküre*. It was originally just an inchoate "twinkle in daddy's eye." Then you will hear something rather unusual, and unusually hard to stage, as Siegfried repeatedly hammers the steel of the sword to increase its strength. Quenching hardens the steel but also makes it brittle, as the carbon alloy has not had time to migrate throughout the iron in the sudden cooling. The older technology of hammering, well known even among smiths of gold, silver, and copper, spreads the carbon through the material and decreases its brittleness. And this carbon migration was an unseen but necessary part of the process, so it took on mysterious and even magical significance for smiths, who were also regarded as sorts of wizards in Norse, Greek, and other mythologies—the Cyclops, Tvastar in the Sanskrit *Rig Veda*, Waylon the Smith, who is Wieland in German, the name of Wagner's oldest grandson. Siegfried hammers the sword to the rhythms we heard so memorably from the enslaved Nibelungs mining for Alberich's wealth in *Das Rheingold* ... DUM-ta-da-DUM-ta-da-DUM-ta-da DUM DUM da DUM-ta-da and so on ... Remember how loud that got when Wotan and Loge were descending into Nibelheim? So it turns out that the orchestral crescendo, complete with eleven live anvils in the current Met production and down the proscenium of the stage, is more than just a terrific gimmick on Wagner's part. It was meant to resonate through the ages—in the score and in our memory. The leitmotif itself spreads through the score like carbon migrating through steel, holding it all together. Siegfried never heard the original form. He didn't need to. The rhythmic theme reveals that the ancient myths are alive and present, in some embedded form, in modern life, in industry and technology. And they're there whether we're consciously aware of them or not. This is one of the most important ways leitmotifs work: they show how we can know and not know things at the same time. The reveal the unseen.

One thing I think Wagner understood perhaps better than anybody is how the parts relate to each other, on the one hand, and to the whole, on the other hand. It was a deep feeling for the π formula, the sacredness of the spaces in between and their relation to each other. This is not only elaborately true for leitmotifs, as we'll see a lot more when they "wrap up," so to speak, in *Götterdämmerung*, but also in every other way too: the characters, the incidents, the instruments in the orchestra, and—here's a way people don't talk about much—the dynamics. The score of the *Ring*, and *Siegfried* in particular, can be very loud but also very soft, even silent. The one informs the other.

It has long been a convention to speak of *Siegfried* as the "scherzo movement" of the *Ring*, as though the four-part drama were a symphony. In fact, it's been such a convention for so long that it bears some reevaluation before we use it again. The scherzo is typically the third movement of a symphony, and is characteristically lighter in tone, a reprieve after the often lugubrious second movement and before the powerful finale. This was especially true in the symphonies of the composer Wagner adored above all and loved to be compared to, Beethoven. The word *scherzo* is Italian for "joke," but also "prank" or "trifle." The scherzo of Beethoven's Second Symphony is actually full of musical jokes that were commented on (sometimes with shock and disapproval) by his contemporaries, while that of his Third Symphony follows directly after the movement that is designated a Funeral March.

Siegfried is certainly the third of four movements, if we think of the *Ring* as a big symphony, but its humorousness can be overhyped. I believe it was less of a laugh riot than Nietzsche thought it was. He was among the first to attach the scherzo appellation to *Siegfried*, so right away we know this is not to be considered humor as any other mortal not named Nietzsche would have defined it. There are indeed amusing moments in it—his cry of *"Das ist kein Mann!"* when he sees the sleeping Brünnhilde being known far and wide—but so there are in *Das Rheingold*. I think the best insight to cull from thinking of *Siegfried* as the scherzo movement is to understand the importance of the lightly scored and even silent passages of the score. Returning again to structure, we look at the heart of the score, the middle of Act II. We know we are meant to look for the heart when hunting for meaning because Siegfried has already told us he will slay the dragon by looking for its heart. As Siegfried lies on the forest floor and the sounds of nature (part of the beautiful Forest Murmurs) die away, he decides to cut a reed and try to imitate the song of a forest bird who seems to be singing to him. Several silent measures appear as Siegfried whittles his reed. It's a weird and wonderful moment, and curiously, I rarely hear anyone in the audience cough during this passage. Of course Siegfried can't make birdsong even after several attempts, the poor oboist in the pit obliging with sad, out of tune whistles. It always gets a few laughs, but even more people like to point to it as a pathetic Teutonic attempt at galumphing humor. I think it's the very quiet and frequently silent heart of the music at the very center of the score that matter most here. It's the true meaning of scherzo. And it soon summons forth the dragon, with his low bassoon underpinnings, and then gets very loud. The next act begins with an absolute river of sound—a moment that rivals the end of *Das Rheingold* for sheer volume.

The orchestral prelude to Act III of *Siegfried* is the crossroads of the *Ring* in every way. Wotan the Wanderer is literally standing at the crossroads, of time as he faces his own future in the form of Siegfried, of geography as he attempts to deflect Siegfried's vector, and every other way. Everything after will be different in a distinct way than what has gone before. The prelude contains reminiscences of what happened, and we can be confident that within those reminiscences lies the blueprint for what will follow. Yet it is a coherent musical unit of its own. It exists both discretely and as a part of everything around it, as we all do. It is like a strand of DNA, or better yet, a quasar, containing all the other moments in it.

Every musical commentator agrees that Wagner was the supreme practitioner of the suspension, the unresolved chord that keeps the listener's ear in an appended state. In a sense, the scores of his complete operas *Tristan und Isolde* and *Parsifal* can each be understood as single suspensions, hours and hours of melody keeping the ear in suspense before finally resolving the chord at the very end that had been opened up in the first measures. But even his single suspensions, as in each of the orchestral chords that mark Brünnhilde's awakening in Act III of tonight's opera, are brilliant suspensions. And so are all his moments that exist by looking both backward and forward, such as we heard layered at the finale of *Das Rheingold* and will hear again in the prelude to Act III tonight. They're all part of his genius for relating parts to the whole, like Tolstoy but in music: musical metonymy. Those suspensions are only glorious in how they prepare you for the climax—that is, in relation to something else. But Wagner always, always has a resolution, a climax, a resolution. His suspensions are not a tease. They are prolongations which allow and demand deeper exploration. There's a big difference. Wagner complained that the Grand Opera of his day depended on "effects without causes." His work never has effects without causes. Wagner's suspensions are the causes of the effects.

In *Siegfried*, these causes and effects penetratingly address the process of discovery: the moment of awakening; the discovery of love; the discovery of fear. And these are all curiously intertwined. Note the upward runs of the harp as Brünnhilde wakes up. They're the mirror image of the descending chords Mime used to try to describe fear to Siegfried in Act I. As much as I admire the beauty of the music when Brünnhilde awakes, it only becomes truly face-melting considered against what we heard before it, even less famous music from uncelebrated passages of the score. The score of the *Ring* really is one massive, holistic achievement. You might just have to break it apart into little bits to see how.

When we compare the music of the character of Siegfried to that of preceding generations, we understand that not only do successive generations express themselves differently through differing technologies, but that each generation carries its own set of fears. Fear might be considered the central issue in this opera, and for this very reason. We can understand the diversity of historic experience between each generation by looking at what they feared. In *Siegfried*, we learn that the monsters and magic that scared our ancestors don't scare us. It's human emotion (love, intimacy, contact, touch) that scares us, the descendants of the proto-humans Siegfried and Brünnhilde.

Love and fear have to be experienced on the micro level in this opera, with its spare cast of characters set apart from everyone else, before we can experience it on the macro level with competing groups of people in the world of politics we will enter in *Götterdämmerung*. Enjoy this moment in time.

Chapter V
About *Götterdämmerung*...and
Everything Else

We have reached the final chapter, we still have a lot to go through. Indeed, everything changes between in the course of *Götterdämmerung*. But more to the point, this trip never really ends. That's the reason it is the *Ring* "Cycle." Every cycle is an entirely new journey just by its context, whether they are trips around the sun—our own or the planet's—or anything else even remotely cyclical. I think that is good news. I find the *Ring* to be life-affirming, and the "End of the World" we are about to experience is actually, if you will allow the expression in this case, a happy ending. And a happier beginning.

Of course, we have a lot of beginning to get through before any talk of endings, and the beginning of *Götterdämmerung* goes back to the beginning of all things, with the famous (or infamous) Norns' scene. Everyone who feels inclined to complain about the structure (and length) of the *Ring* will reflexively bitch about the Norns. They are "dreary" (Anna Russell's word). They go on too long (about eleven minutes, a mere blip in *Ring*-time). They tell you the whole story all over again. This bad attitude toward the Norns is only exacerbated by those who are overly committed to the Retro Theory of the *Ring*'s composition. The notion is that Wagner had to put the Norns in to tell the backstory, but then wrote no fewer than three prequels. This much can be confirmed by history, but the next step in extrapolating this point of view is when it becomes untenable, which is the notion that Wagner then refused to edit himself even after he had written three whole prequels. He was just so in love with his own writing that he could not bear to cut out eleven minutes of music even though he had replaced them with hours of stage drama. As much as this is believable in the context of Wagner the Megalomaniac, I find it hard

to believe regarding Wagner the Theatrical Genius. So looking at the
Norns the way we are looking at everything here in this go-round, we have
to ask "What if he didn't accidentally leave them in as a sort of vestige—
like a lyrical appendix— because he forgot that they were there, or
something? What, then, can we actually learn about this piece from these
dreary characters?"

First off, they don't really tell us the whole story all over again.
There's actually almost nothing they say that is a representation of what
we have seen on stage. They are looking back, though, and they do make
reference to Loge having been summoned by Wotan's spear to burn
around Brünnhilde's rock, but they tell it from Loge's point of view. And
they give contrary information to at least one thing we have heard Wotan
explain differently—twice: how he lost his eye. Here, it was the price he
paid for drinking at the spring under the World Ash Tree. In *Das
Rheingold*, he told Fricka how he had given up his eye as the cost of
marrying her (although he does not explain how that came to pass). Later
he told Siegfried that the eye which the boy rudely asks about is now in
Siegfried looking back at him, which is just creepy and weird. But the
point is that all these stories exist as memories, and they become more and
more fanciful as time progresses. Furthermore, the Norns either give
details which had been missing in the previous accounts of the eye story,
or they just make up stuff. The process continues as they give many other
details about the world that has passed into time already, and we never
know if they're important missing details, or just making up stories. The
Norns are in fact the institution of mythology itself, which must be dealt
with in itself before we can move on to the modern world. Interestingly,
one of the last things they say—all three of them, together, which as you
know is very rare in the late Wagnerian way of writing music—is *"Zu End'
ewiges Wissen,"* "Thus ends our eternal wisdom." This again seems to
make no sense. But it makes no sense in a methodical way. It bookmarks
the end of something that began with an analogous time-warp, when
Wotan woke up and declared in *Das Rheingold* "the eternal work is
finished!" An era of interpreting time in a warped way is coming to a close.
The era of linear time is beginning and will triumph for a while, at least
until Einstein and Picasso and some others arrived. The Norns can see

what humans could only begin to fathom two generations after Wagner: space, and its corollary, time, are both curved. A straightforward narrative must be cyclical.

The majority of the stories that the Norns relate, about Wotan visiting the spring and paying for a drink with an eye, about chopping up the withered World Ash Tree (known elsewhere as Yggdrasil) and using the wood to surround Valhalla so it can burn down in the general conflagration at Ragnarok, and so forth, are entirely new and among the most intriguing and colorful in the *Ring*. They are, I think, what a lot of people assume most of the *Ring* will be about—the most fanciful of stories deriving from the ancient Norse. I wish they had more time on stage. And I'm not the only one. The late Father M. Owen Lee, a long-time commentator on Wagner and an academic specialist in Greek classics, had a lot to say on this subject. Father Lee, as he was known, felt that, far from being too long, the *Ring* was actually missing an entire opera. There should have been a prequel to *Das Rheingold* called *The World Ash Tree* to show us the rise of Wotan and the passing of the previous era of the Erda-based, matriarchal authority. I agree entirely. Besides providing us with a chance to revel in the colorful scenes merely referred to by the Norns, this would have given us a clearer sense of the Age of the Gods, from beginning to end, as one more epoch in the succession of eras that form the concatenation of The Story of Everything, just another Karmic Cycle. But it is a bit churlish to complain about the *Ring* being too short—especially in a discussion of *Götterdämmerung*.

I think that what's important about the Norns is what they tell us about the evolution of human storytelling. And they do launch, in a very curious way, one of the most massive single chunks of theater ever conceived—the Prologue and Act One of *Götterdämmerung*. There will be a Siegfried/Brünnhilde duet, a symphonic interlude (the "Rhine Journey"), a scene in the Hall of the Gibichungs, an evil monologue for the piece's villain, a sort of reverse symphonic interlude, a confrontation between Brünnhilde and her sister Waltraute, and a final difficult (in every sense) scene between Siegfried (disguised, in some fashion, as another character) and Brünnhilde. In other words, the complex second acts in *Die Walküre* and *Siegfried*, with their half-dozen separate-but-related scenes of confrontations, are placed up front in this opera and expanded in both length and number of characters. It's over two hours without a break.

How else is this opera different from what we have already experienced? I mentioned the Hall of the Gibichungs. This is another first of sorts, and an important one. It is the first actual architecture in the *Ring*. We hear about Valhalla and its construction in *Das Rheingold*, and in theory we see it dimly, surrounded by clouds, in the distance (as through a mirror darkly) but we never enter it. It is more concept than construct. In *Die Walküre* we have Hunding's hut, built around a tree, and in *Siegfried* we have Mime's forge in a cave, but both of those are attempts to find a human place within nature. They are not buildings. Hunding's hut involved some woodworking, and Mime's cave involves blacksmithing, both of which are sequential steps in the evolution of the modern order, but the Hall of the Gibichungs is actual architecture. This is the modern patriarchal political order enshrined. And it is in the Hall that we find an abundance of other signs of that order. The very first words we hear there involve fame—that is, concern for reputation among other humans. Gunther says *"Nun hör, Hagen, sage mir, Held: sitz'ich herrlich am Rhein?"* Or, "Now hark, Hagen, tell me, Hero ... am I sitting lordly on the Rhine?" Wait, what? Maybe better to say, "Am I considered noble along the Rhine?" In other words, "How are my ratings in our market share?" So, in the civilized architectural world of manipulated (rather than accommodated) nature, you have façades (literally) and everything that goes along with them. Besides fame, there are, for example, spurious identities, when Siegfried dons the magic Tarnhelm and masquerades as Gunther. The Tarnhelm had never before been used to pass as another human, least of all *by* a human. In *Das Rheingold*, the Tarnhelm had been used either for invisibility or to become a scary beast, and it remains so until Fafner's death in *Siegfried*. But in the civilized world, the power to deceive takes on more possibilities. As human love and touch instilled fear in characters who had never before been afraid of the old gods and monsters, so now in the more recognizable world will specifically human deceptions and "false fronts" prove even more perilous.

In the Hall of the Gibichungs, we are also confronted right away with a new level of social ritual. We have toasts. Siegfried drinks to

Brünnhilde. This is a first in the *Ring*. Any other composer/librettist would have had Siegmund say something "toasty" to Sieglinde in Act I of *Die Walküre*, but it was all unspoken (and their attraction was communicated to us by an unforgettable solo cello line that later became a sung love theme, "*Du bist der Lenz*," or "You are the Spring"). In the older world of *Die Walküre*, like in the Sanskrit language, words and deeds are identical. There was no need for Siegmund to recite a formulaic declaration of love to Sieglinde because his commitment to her was genuine and unquestionable and because she was actually right there. In *Götterdämmerung*, words function more as monuments to remote ideals that are probably corrupt if not outright dead. The world, *this* world, is getting old. Siegfried's toast to Brünnhilde only serves as a prelude to his betrayal of her, shortly to follow. So, too, does his oath of blood brotherhood with Gunther. He will be accused of betraying that shortly as well—and his solemn word counts for nothing to the public. Why would it?

So the system of musical themes known as leitmotifs now take on additional meaning as words and deeds also take on additional, often unspoken, sometimes deceptive, meanings. We see this in a big way in Act II, which begins with a weird Alberich scene that may or may not be Hagen's dream (it probably is, unless Hagen is talking in his sleep—a feat that is of course not unthinkable for the son of a guy who sang and even sneezed underwater). Alberich tells his son to remain true to their original plan of world domination, hating the happy, and all manner of other dastardly supervillain activities. He tells him "*Sei treu*," "be true" (keep the faith, remain steady) in a two-note descending phrase, a minor second. Alberich repeats the second note and word, "*treu*" rather mysteriously. It echoes in the orchestra and is soon repeated as a horn call. Hagen will arouse himself from one his many stupors and call all the vassals with a series of bellowing calls, "*Hei-Ho!*" that are not only on the same two notes as Alberich's "*Sei treu*," but also a shadowy half step of Siegfried's forging cry. Hagen's thrilling "call to the vassals" results in them rushing to him, and we have the first chorus in the entire *Ring*. And if all goes right, it will blow your face off. The chorus responds to him with variations of his two-note minor second, his "*Hei-ho*."

We already heard in *Das Rheingold* how important two notes can be, when Donner summoned the clouds away from Valhalla with a notable leap of a fourth in the scale, "*Hei da!*" (Kaiser Wilhelm II used that theme for his limo horn, among other Wagnerian embellishments in his life and reign). And of course, shortly after that, we hear Wotan augment the leap of a fourth into a fifth when he gets the "idea" to plant a sword somewhere (even though we don't know he's thinking about a sword yet, theoretically). And another upward fifth will launch the actual Siegfried motif, so closely related to the sword motif as to suggest the two are essentially identical (Siegfried plays both the sword and his own motifs on his horn, back to back, after the grand "silence" in Act II of *Siegfried*). He uses the actual phrase "*Hei-ho!*" And Alberich's downward "*Sei treu*" (which becomes Hagen's "*Hei-Ho,*" which then becomes the vassals' response) will be directly contrasted with Siegfried's upward phrase in Act III, when they become a study of Death vs. Life (the former depicting an old idea going limp, the latter being a new idea springing forth, and more on which in a moment). It's not just a story of who does bad things to whom in this (or any good) opera: it's an epic encounter of natures in conflict—matter vs. anti-matter, if you will. Right here, however, what matters is the vector from Alberich planting an idea in Hagen's dream that he audibly amplifies and which gets answered by the vassals. Behold the true nature of politics in our modern world. People say things and they become political slogans. Later on, people don't even know the backstory of what they're saying, because it was planted by our antecedents either in our dreams or in our DNA (which are perhaps the same thing, in some way). But these origins are there whether we acknowledge them or not, and they are important. Backstory is not bad dramaturgy. It's essential socio-political psychology.

It's also an important ingredient of any historical study, and *Götterdämmerung* firmly moves us along from the mythological world to something much closer to the world of history. This observation means we now have to talk about sources once again. Other than the Norns' scene and the actual fire-and-flood of the finale (that is, the very beginning and the very end), the direct source of this opera is not the Norse myths but the medieval German epic poem, the *Nibelungenlied*. And although the Norse sagas that Wagner used (especially the *Volsunga Saga*) have many of the same characters as the *Nibelungenlied*, or versions of them, it is mostly as they are depicted in the *Nibelungenlied* that we meet them or re-meet them in *Götterdämmerung*. Thus Brünnhilde acts a lot more like a proud medieval princess here than she did in her previous incarnations, while Siegfried, who basically knew nothing in the previous opera, now suddenly knows how to sail a boat, propose a toast, and swear an oath after what must have been an extraordinary night of sex with his bride. (We actually don't know how long it was, but it is a metaphorical single night if not a chronological one.) Therefore, if we're going to understand about *Götterdämmerung* that which we tried to understand about each of these operas (namely, how it is a part of the whole and how it is a different work), we need to look at the differences between the Norse sagas and the *Nibelungenlied* and other sources.

Wait… "other sources"? Yes and no. Another ancient mythology (if we may call it that for the moment) present in *Götterdämmerung* is that of India, or at least (again) the mid-nineteenth century understanding of the ancient mythology of India. The very ancient Puranas and many sources since then tell us that Lord Vishnu, in his tenth incarnation as Kalki, will come on a white horse, brandishing a sword against his nemesis, the chaos-loving, peace-hating demon Kali (not the goddess Kali … this one is male). This will begin a general apocalypse ending this entire fourth (fourth!) cycle of existence, the corrupt Kali Yuga (yuga = aeon, era) that we live in.

Kalki, then, is a prototype of many familiar figures from other mythologies: he is Siegfried (and the relativity of the names Kalki and Kali points to the deadly bond between Siegfried and Hagen that we heard in the music, and also to their "fathers" Alberich and Wotan—who, in the opera *Siegfried* curiously went so far as to identify himself as the "Licht Alberich," the "Alberich of Light"). Kalki is even a little bit Jesus Christ, who brandishes a sword and combats an archenemy on the Last Day. But this Hindu rendition of *"Das Ende"* hovers close by our tale for several other reasons. First off, it is older than all the others, and therefore has a certain authority. But more important for our purposes is its Indian identity. The budding science of comparative philology in Wagner's time

(Nietzsche was a professor of philology, let's remember) was perfectly obsessed right then with the anthropological implications stemming from the discovery of a common source between Indic and Modern European languages. This is the theoretical language called Proto-Indo-European. Most notable was the idea, especially perpetrated by the French racial theorist Count Arthur de Gobineau, that there was a race of humans behind this language: the Aryans, whose name means "noble." The Aryans must have, they thought, "conquered" lands from Ireland (the Irish language also descends from Proto-Indo-European and even the name Eire might be—and was certainly thought by nineteenth-century philologists to have been—a linguistic variation on the term Arya, as modern "Iran" is known to be). Also, note the importance of the word *"Ehre,"* German for "honor" and presumed to be derived from the prototype for Aryan, in everything from the libretto of the *Ring* to the motto of the Hitler Youth, *"Blut und Ehre,"* or "blood and honor." (Of all Octavian's many names in Strauss's *Der Rosenkavalier*, the only German one is Ehrenreich, "rich in honor.")

The theorized race of Aryans was understood to be very tall and very blond and very noble, flowing in all directions from a theorized home in Central Asia and kicking butt on all the short, dark, weasely "inferiors" in their path, from Ireland to Scandinavia right across to the indigenous Dravidian peoples of India. The *Ring*'s libretto, with its constant references to the Volsungs, Siegmund, and Sieglinde, as a *Geschlecht*, a "species" or even a "race," makes a lot more sense if we consider this racial understanding of proto-history. In reality, the "Aryans" weren't a race or any sort of bloodline, and we have learned that there a lot of ways for language and mythology to spread besides conquest. Modern cultural studies are almost (but unfortunately not quite) unanimous in understanding that, even in ancient times, "Aryan" was used as a cultural-linguistic, rather than racial, category. This racial misconception of Aryanism was based on erroneous readings of the *Rig Veda*, along with a lot of wishful thinking among the "fair" races, and has been disproved many times—and yet, it was powerful to Wagner at the time he was writing the *Ring*. He later rejected Gobineau's theories, when he returned to work on *Parsifal*, because they did not allow for the power of Jesus Christ (who, we are told, transcends East and West, Male and Female,

Greek and Jew) to overcome racial division. This was the philosophical
volte-face that made Nietzsche rabidly despise Wagner for the rest of that
philologist's embittered, unhappy life. But what's important right now is
the wide-ranging impression of comparative mythology that was swirling
in Wagner's imagination at the time, and the spectrum of implications,
from sublime to toxic, that it includes.

However much Gobineau may have wanted the *Rig Veda* to be a
version of history, we must categorize its presence in our present tale as
mythological. Then there is the final work to speak of as a source for
Götterdämmerung, which actually contains a lot of history in it: The
Nibelungenlied is clearly more historical than the Norse works or the *Rig
Veda*. That is, it relates versions of historical events more closely to how
they must have happened than the more removed sagas and vedas. There
actually was a Gunther of Burgundy and a Brynnhild of Austrasia (which
was neither Austria nor Asia but more like our modern Belgium). And in
the *Nibelungenlied* we read about Kriemhild, (Gutrune Gibich in this
opera), who ends up marrying no less historical a personage than Attila the
Hun in Part 2—because believe it or not, everything we are about to see in
the opera tonight between the Norns and the end of the world is merely
Part 1 of the *Nibelungenlied*. From Gunther and Brynnhild and especially
Attila, we can place the events of the story—even those which are obvious
and fanciful inventions—in a historical time frame. This is the era of the
decline and fall of the Roman Empire, which is not incidentally concurrent
with what we call the Age of Migrations. The Burgundians were a
Germanic tribe "invited" by the Romans to cross the Rhine and settle in
lands of the necrotic Roman Empire. This Gunther, we are told, had a stash
of gold which he hid in the Rhine and which was never found. And the
Burgundians, who would have invaded anyway because they were driven
forth by another migratory warrior nation, the Huns, were sometimes
allied with and sometimes at war with the Romans and especially the great
Roman general Flavius Aëtius, whom, incidentally, we meet as Ezio in
Verdi's opera *Attila*, which, incidentally, also mentions Wotan, "Vodano,"
and deals with the semi-mythical founding of the sublime city of Venice
amid fire and flood.

What's important for us beyond the fact of the *Nibelungenlied*'s historicity is the moment it depicts. It is a transitional one, from an old order (the Roman Empire) to a new order (the Middle Ages, feudalism, chivalry, etc.). We remember that there is something inherently fertile to the storyteller about such moments: we remember the mythological gold mine of the Trojan War and its aftermath, and the Norse commemorating their transition from subsistence-level tribes to warrior nations as they learned how to forge steel and build ships. This time of the fall of the Roman Empire is also the era of that supreme source of subsequent European myth and legend, King Arthur. A lot of magic-sword-based fire-and-water death-and-renewal was going in the fifth century in those parts of the world.

Since we know that the past contains large chunks of previous pasts (like leitmotifs) embedded within it, we can find even older history murkily buried in some of the stories here. Siegfried himself is constantly referred to in this opera as a famous hero of many deeds, yet all we've actually seen is him slaying a dragon. (Admittedly, quite a deed, but no one saw him do it, and yet everyone in Gibichungland knows about it…) So we know right away that Siegfried is a type, one who appears in several different retellings of stories, and is meant to be understood in this symbolic, multiple-identities sort of way. The Siegfried of the various medieval stories may also be a fuzzily remembered reference to Arminius of the Roman annals of Tacitus and elsewhere, known in Germany as Hermann, who inflicted the crushing defeat on the Roman Army at the Battle of Teutoberg Forest in 9 A.D., which sent the forces of Rome flying back over to "their" (i.e., the Western) side of the Rhine for the remaining four centuries of the empire. This was considered a pivotal event in European history—if you ever read or saw Robert Graves's *I, Claudius*, you'll remember Augustus Caesar obsessing like a spoiled brat about getting back the Imperial Eagles (battle standards) lost at Teutoberg Forest. The "dragon" that Siegfried slew might be a reference the Roman legions defeated by Herrmann, presumed invincible because of their "scaly" armor and their phalanxes tightly formed under their overlapping shields (called *tortugae*, tortoises), which could not be pierced from without except into their "heart" through some soft underbelly (from underneath?). This is certainly what people thought in the nineteenth century, and that point of view must have pervaded Wagner's thinking.

The Rhine ... it keeps coming back in our story, and it keeps coming back in legend and in history. It had long formed the boundary between the Roman and the Germanic world, and Teutoberg Forest sealed that boundary even after the fall of Rome. It still exists, if not always legally, then certainly mentally. It is the sacred boundary between Latin, Catholic Europe and Germanic, Protestant Europe. The West bank of the Rhine, even in Germany, has maintained a connection to Roman Catholicism—especially its largest city, Cologne, a Roman city. And the West bank has been repeatedly claimed by France in wars and diplomacy: Louis XIV, the French revolutionaries, their nationalist heirs in Wagner's time, Napoleons I and III, and then the victorious French Republic after World War I. It was during a diplomatic crisis initiated by France's prime minister Louis-Adolphe Thiers that Germany promulgated the popular song "*Die Wacht am Rhein*," "The Watch on the Rhine," which appears in the film *Casablanca* as the song the German soldiers sing in Rick's Café Americain to trigger an oppositional group-sing of "*La Marseillaise*." That film, released just after American and British troops landed in the French North Africa of its setting, encapsulates two millennia of hostility in one minute of discordant musical antagonism. Wagner happened to loathe the popular song "*Die Wacht am Rhein*" as a product of low musical taste. When he heard that German soldiers were singing it on their way to the Franco-Prussian War, he said he hoped they would be defeated, a cynical quip from a less than charming man who proceeded to urge Germany's leaders to destroy Paris. But he was not above respecting the sentiment in the song, and even quoting it in a sense, since the chorus of the song says "*fest steht und treu die Wacht, die Wacht am Rhein*" ("Strong and true stands the watch on the Rhine"). Besides Alberich's "*Sei treu*," Hagen describes himself at one point (with no one listening, so for our benefit) "*Hier sitz' ich zur Wacht, wahren den Hof, wehre die Halle dem Feind*" ("Here I sit on watch, guarding the house, defending the hall from the foe"). There were many depictions of "Hagen's Watch on the Rhine" printed up during and after Wagner's lifetime. The Rhine is very, very important in mythical, legendary, and political ways.

Because there is more history in *Götterdämmerung*, there is more *Götterdämmerung* in history. And history gets ugly sometimes. Siegfried's sword was understood in Wagner's time as a clear metaphor for the German Empire, the Second Reich, which contained the basic material of the original sword (the First Reich, the Holy Roman Empire, discussed at some length in Wagner's *Lohengrin* and at more length in his *Die Meistersinger von Nürnberg*). The broken pieces of the original work (the 300-plus constituent states of the late Holy Roman Empire) had to be further "smashed to bits" and melted down in fire before they could be refashioned anew and tempered in cool, solidifying water to become a potent new entity. Siegfried's actually useful sword, as opposed to Siegmund's ineffective one given and then destroyed by Wotan symbolizes the modern nation state of the German Empire—disencumbered of its Holiness and purified of its Romanness.

The symbolism was not lost on united Germany's leaders. In both world wars, the Germans created defensive lines facing France called the Siegfried Line. In World War I, German offensive operations included military plans codenamed "Alberich" and "Hagen," the latter of which appositely involved a flanking attack designed to strike the British forces defending Northern France from behind, just as Hagen stabs Siegfried in the back in Act III of *Götterdämmerung*. When Germany lost the war, its generals, and later Adolf Hitler in *Mein Kampf*, promulgated the myth that German armies had not really been defeated, but that their heroic efforts had been betrayed from within. The term they used was "stab in the back" (*Dolchstoss*) in direct reference to Siegfried's demise. Old myths die hard. In fact, they don't die at all.

The interpretive excesses of the Second Reich—the German Empire that existed from 1871 to 1918—became the atrocities of the Third Reich. In addition to building their own Siegfried Line to defend the Rhineland against France, the Nazis outdid their predecessors even before World War II when their air raids obliterated the Spanish town of Guernica—commemorated in Picasso's famous painting—in the euphoniously Wagnerian name of "Operation Feuerzauber," or "Magic Fire" (as in the finale of *Die Walküre*). And that was just the tip of the Wagnerian iceberg. While archeology and every other science disproved the relation of the Proto-Indo-European language to any "noble" light-skinned race of Aryans—and even disproved the existence of the Aryans as a racial group—the meta-myth was kept alive by theoreticians such as, notably, Houston Stewart Chamberlain. This individual was the British-born racial theorist, anti-Semite, tutor (no less) of Adolf Hitler, inspirer of Joseph Goebbels, and most *imperfect* Wagnerite ever, who was even married to Wagner's daughter Eva. The swastika itself became the Nazi symbol because it was an Aryan symbol (Swastik = Sanskrit "conducive to well-being").

Now, before we get too smug about these schmucks having coopted all this mythology back then, take a moment to consider that it is happening still, and louder than it has in a long time. This is true as well for the vedic mythology among Hindu nationalists, but also well beyond India too. The notion that there is a Master Aryan Race responsible for all the benefits of civilization that must dominate the shifty darker races for the inferiors' own guidance has currency in many places in the world today, including in our own country's Alt-Right and its apologists in our very own government. Not only don't old myths die, neither do their misinterpretations—or their lies.

The vedas and the epics of India do contain the seeds of racial domination theory, if one is committed to finding them. However, the bigger and more howlingly obvious way to read them is as transcendent masterpieces of mythopoetics. And, like the vedas, it was never imperative to read the *Ring* in the way the racists have—not even in the 1930s and 1940s. If there was an Operation Feuerzauber, there was also an Operation Valkyrie conceived by those German officers who tried to assassinate Hitler and take over the government in 1944. Even before that, in the 1930s, we remember Friedelind Wagner, the anti-Nazi Wagner so unlike her Aunt Eva and Uncle Houston and many of the others, staring at the Nazi leadership during performances of the *Ring*, aghast that they could think this whole epic was about anything other than their own self-defeating crimes. "How can you possibly be processing your conclusions from the evidence we are both looking at?" It's something we experience every day in our current politics. *How* you read a text is everything, and everything is a text.

I think the mistake that the propagandists made in their reading of the *Ring* was in being literal, which is a form of superficiality. Literalism is just as big a problem here as it can be in interpreting religious texts and political constitutions. The Nazis and their ilk were being literally literal: working with the libretto only, and this work is more than the libretto. Every opera is. I am not saying, as some do, that the music justifies the libretto, much less that you should "enjoy the pretty music and ignore everything else." You couldn't even if you wanted to. I'm saying the music is the true story in an opera, and the libretto can be an aid in understanding the score. It is never the story itself. You will run into the same problem in interpreting Puccini's *Madama Butterfly*, or many others. Those characters who read as *victims* in a libretto can become *victors* within the context of the entire opera. The music tells a different story, a deeper one, than the words alone. Suicide, for example, is often the mark of victory in opera—certainly it is so for Butterfly, Aida, Brünnhilde, Tosca, and most others. It's even a form of redemption for Verdi's Otello, if not a victory.

You can hear victory in the conclusion of Siegfried's Funeral Music. Those fragments of leitmotifs that indicated Siegfried and his now (dormant) sword are contrasted with Hunding's minor descending two-note leitmotif and also with two extremely loud (the entire orchestra thundering *fortississimo*, as loud as possible) iterations of the same note, the greatest musical description of death in history. The finality of death is undeniable in this depiction—and yet, oddly, not even this encapsulation of the finality of death is the last word in the Funeral Music. A simple, final new formulation of two notes moving up the scale tells us everything we could know about the victory over death—Siegfried's victory, specifically. It is the reverse of Alberich's "*Sei treu,*" the Will to Death (in Schopenhauer's term). He is definitely dead. But he wins. He rises again even as he lies lifeless.

Since music is not literal by definition, so the leitmotifs are a non-literal form of history—received information from the past transformed by present understanding. What we can see, that the propagandists failed to see, is that the *Ring* is more than political history. It is human evolutionary history, which even includes in it the history of humans regarding their own evolution. And evolution and our understanding of it are cyclical, as is everything else.

So where do we go in *Götterdämmerung*—the goal, so to speak, of the entire *Ring*? How do we find a takeaway that is neither as toxic, nor as moribund, nor as frankly flat-out irrelevant as those of a century ago now seem to us? George Bernard Shaw, as we talked about at some length, suggested the *Ring* was a journey back in music history time, beginning with revolutionary "music drama" in *Das Rheingold* and ending with disappointingly traditional Grand Opera in *Götterdämmerung*. Perhaps what was important for us about Shaw's point of view is not so much the actual musical forms he cited to support his retroactive view of the *Ring*, but rather the mid-nineteenth century's view of *how* to interpret these things. And along with a critique of the bourgeois audience's preference for rousing tunes over profound musicalized speech comes a critique of all superficial arts consumption, a critique we can heartily commend.

If this is so, then there's nothing wrong with Grand Opera, per se. The problem was in Shaw's retrogressive contemporary audience. This moves into realizing that once again we are not only talking about the observed but the observer as well—us. We understand Heisenberg's Uncertainty Principle in an even bigger way when we remember that the act of observation changes not only the observed but, as the leading Brünnhilde of our day, Christine Goerke has said, that it changes the observer as well. And the racialists and the Third Reich showed us that the change is not always for the better, not by a long shot. We play an active role in determining how the evolution—our own personal one and the universe's—will play out, even if we chose to do or to think nothing at all. And if this is a mind-blowing variation on the Uncertainty Principle, and it is effected most visibly in our reactions to this single, massive work (i.e., which of the character's point of view within the story we will use as an example to formulate our own points of view of the story), then that is a mind-blowing variation on the mind-blowing variation of the greatest mind-blowing principle of modernity. The *Ring*, as it turns out, is Live Action Role Play, and the game is The Entire Universe.

If Wagner's intent, or that of his disciples, was to use the *Ring* to kill off traditional opera once and for all, then we can see from the vantage point of history that they all failed miserably. On the contrary, the *Ring*, by demanding we play an active role in its own meaning, has taught us a better way to experience opera—all opera, even such "trash" as Donizetti (per Wagner—I adore Donizetti and so does any sentient being, and so deep down did Wagner). Unless you are lucky enough to go to Bayreuth, you are not in a special festival house in the middle of nowhere. You are at a definitive opera house. The *Ring* did not kill Grand Opera. It came to stand for it. The institution of Grand Opera is telegraphed in an instant visual to any modern person by nothing better than the hoary cliché of the overly breast-plated, blond-plaited warrior goddess brandishing a spear and hollering at impossible levels of volume—none other than Brünnhilde.

Anna Russell enforced that notion when she noted penetratingly, speaking of Siegmund's immoral, illicit seduction of his married twin sister in Act I of *Die Walküre*, "But that's the beauty of Grand Opera— you can get away with anything so long as you sing it!" This is, after all, another way of saying that singing something changes the fundamental meaning of a thing that is merely said. Russell also looked at the end of the whole cycle and noted the music at the very end that we had heard at the very beginning—the Rhine Maidens and so forth. Russell exclaimed in mock shock, "We're right back where we started seventeen hours ago!" So we are reminded of the "cycle" aspect of the *Ring*, but we know we are not quite where we had begun seventeen hours previously because we are learning a new definition of circularity. It is clear that the next age will not be a case of Pete Townsend's "meet the new boss, same as the old boss" firstly because the music tells us it will not. We know that even if we were to draw a perfect circle in space, we could never draw the same one twice because time and space would have moved under it, making it something else. And we remember Joyce DiDonato's observation that singing the exact same notes in the final verse of a baroque "da capo" aria would still be a variation on the first verse's iteration because having it heard it once has changed our ears somehow. So instead of being *right* back where we started, it is more a case of what my grandmother used to call "going all around the block to get to the house next door." If all birth is rebirth, per Norman O. Brown, then no new birth could ever be entirely new, but also no new rebirth could ever be entirely not old. Every brand-spanking new thing contains within it something old and presumed lost, and that old thing contained within it something even older, like a leitmotif.

If we don't read the classics of India as genocidal white supremacists do, then we see much greater lessons. Vishnu the Preserver rests on Shesha, the thousand-headed serpent that is both Vishnu's servant and his manifestation. The name Shesha means "that which remains," because Shesha is Ananta, Eternal—and who hasn't seen the Eternal represented in many cultures as a snake (cf. the ouroboros)? Creation cannot proceed out of nothing, so Ananta Shesha is that which remains after the apparently total immolation of *"Das Ende"*—just as there is always a small amount of desire left, perhaps in a charred and drenched but somehow purified state, even after the desired object has been attained. And this Shesha is Vishnu too, or contains Vishnu in it, ready to appear to us in a concatenation of avatars until creation is destroyed once again at the end of the next age.

There is evolution, but it is very, very slow in its cycles. We cannot be exactly where we were because time and space have moved under the perfect circle. You cannot step into the same river twice—not even *this* river. Even if we went all around the block to get to the house next door, we would still be, in fact, next door. The era ends but a bit of it remains and a better if still highly imperfect world, subject to its own cycles of purification, awaits. Kalki Yuga. Ragnarok. *Götterdämmerung.* Sunrise, every single day. As Ovid and the Vedas knew, the core truths may be immutable, but the bodies change and might even become these bodies we ourselves inhabit. The whole difference from one to another is in the *how*.

I opened this book by writing that we should think big and listen hard. You don't have to see this work the way I do, but I insist you see it in a state of amazement, like I do, to experience it as a vital, transcendental, and evergreen masterpiece—and also perhaps to do yourself a good deed of renewal as well. We will all survive the general conflagration and inundation at the end, and maybe, just maybe, we will survive Ragnarok like something out of Vishnu's dream of dissolution and recreation. That is, you might just find yourself a little better off, and more essentially *you* than you had been before the soundings of *Das Rheingold*.

Index

CPSIA information can be obtained
at www.ICGtesting.com
Printed in the USA
LVHW071646250822
726872LV00009B/332